WITH PAUL AT SEA

with **Paul** at Sea

Learning from the Apostle Who
Took the Gospel from Land to Sea

Linford Stutzman

 CASCADE *Books* · Eugene, Oregon

WITH PAUL AT SEA
Learning from the Apostle Who Took the Gospel from Land to Sea

Cascade Books
An Imprint of Wipf and Stock Publishers
199 W. 8th Ave., Suite 3
Eugene, OR 97401

www.wipfandstock.com

ISBN 13: 978-1-61097-425-7

Cataloging-in-Publication data:

Stutzman, Linford

With Paul at sea : learning from the apostle who took the gospel from land to sea / Linford Stutzman

xviii + 170 p. ; 23 cm. Includes bibliographical references.

ISBN 13: 978-1-61097-425-7

1. Paul, the Apostle, Saint—Travel. 2. Mediterranean Region—Description and travel. I. Title.

BS2505 S85 2012

Manufactured in the U.S.A.

To the Jews, and also to the Greeks, Palestinians, Turks, Lebanese, Syrians, and the international sailing community who have made the Mediterranean Sea the world's most fascinating body of water.

To sons David and Jon, explorers of a changing world, and experimenters with the good news of the kingdom of God.

Contents

"Three times I was shipwrecked; for a night and a day I was adrift at sea; on frequent journeys, in danger from rivers . . . danger at sea. I spent a night and a day in the open sea, have been constantly on the move. I have been . . . in danger at sea."

—*Paul, writing to the Christians*
in the port city of Corinth (2 Cor 11:25b–26)

Preface

IN 2004–5 MY WIFE, Janet, and I spent fifteen months aboard *SailingActs*, an old thirty-three-foot sailboat that we had bought in Greece for the purpose of following Paul's sea journeys in the Mediterranean. During that voyage we sailed over four thousand miles, visiting all thirty-seven harbors and fifty-four cities mentioned in Acts to which Paul traveled. I learned to know Paul in completely new ways on that voyage by sailing the unpredictable Mediterranean Sea, viewing the Roman Empire from sea level, traveling at the speed of Paul, experiencing details of Paul's travels described in Acts, and meeting the colorful descendants of people who, around the middle of the first century, might have eagerly accepted Paul and his message. Or tried to kill him.

To follow Paul on the Mediterranean had been a dream of mine for years and finally had become possible thanks to a sabbatical from Eastern Mennonite University where I teach. This would be no ordinary sabbatical. Even before the sabbatical officially began Janet and I gradually realized that we were not taking a sabbatical; it was taking us. For although we had lived cross-culturally for years and had traveled extensively on five continents, this time we were preparing to live on the unpredictable, unstable, beautiful, and precarious Mediterranean Sea among people who seemed to have taken on some of its characteristics over the millennia.

In March of 2004 we purchased the *Aldebaran*, a twenty-five-year-old Westerly 33, a sturdy but severely neglected British-built sailing ketch, from a retired sea captain in Volos, Greece. In May, I flew to Athens, drove 250 miles north to Volos, moved aboard the *Aldebaran* moored on the city dock directly across the street from busy sidewalk cafes and chic coffee shops. There I began the arduous and expensive six-week task of restoring and outfitting the old vessel for the roughly four-thousand-mile sea voyage, clearing the bureaucratic and legal hurdles of buying a boat in Greece, changing the name, procuring insurance and permissions, and redocumenting the vessel in the United States. On June 18, Janet and I loosened the mooring lines on the almost ready, newly renamed *SailingActs* and eased out of the harbor in Volos, pointing her bow toward the island of Samos across the Aegean where we would intersect with Paul's sea routes and begin following them ourselves. Like Paul leaving Antioch's harbor, Seleucia, in AD 47, we had no idea of what we would be facing.[1]

We saw and experienced what Paul and the pagans[2] would have as they sailed the Mediterranean. We were surprised by the suddenness and ferocity of the storms. We too went without sleep, dreaded the first unavoidable night passage, anchored in unfamiliar harbors among the islands of the Aegean, sailed into the splendid ports of bustling ancient cities, and were vulnerable to the moods of petty governmental officials. Like Paul, we met and appreciated generous and caring Greeks, Turks, Palestinians, Cypriots, and Israelis. In addition we met international sailors, Christians, Muslims, Jews, and pagans, appreciated their expertise, and enjoyed their company and hospitality.

As with many of my generation raised in devote Christian families—Mennonite in my case—and immersed in the world of the Bible from childhood, I had been familiar with Paul the missionary and theologian for my entire life. But sailing with Paul for fifteen months on that sabbatical we became personally acquainted with Paul the explorer, Paul the experimenter. We learned to experientially appreciate the creative genius, the bold and daring innovation, and the unflagging commitment of Paul, the world's first or at least the most famous missionary to the pagan, non-Jewish population of the Roman Empire around the Mediterranean. In subsequent years I have returned each summer to the Mediterranean and

---

1. The complete story of this voyage is available in my book *Sailing Acts*.

2. "Pagan," as I will use the word throughout the book, refers to the tremendous variety of polytheistic religious peoples of the Mediterranean and the ancient Near East. Within both the Old and New Testaments, a variety of descriptive categories such as "nations," "heathen," "Greeks," "Gentiles" are used to differentiate the Jewish monotheists from their polytheistic neighbors. I will use "pagan" in this way.

SailingActs to continue learning from the seaman Paul. On these learning voyages I am often accompanied by undergraduate or seminary students, an arrangement that provides additional insight into the travel conditions aboard small cargo ships in the first century.

For example, I recently spent two weeks aboard a fifty-five-foot schooner with approximately two hundred fifty square feet of living space in which fifteen strangers making up the class and crew cooked, ate, slept, studied, showered, and toileted. I even shared a bunk with a twenty-one-year-old seminary student, a kind of modern equivalent to Paul being chained to a Roman soldier on his voyage to Rome. Compared with sea voyages on the Mediterranean in the first century however, this was sheer luxury.

Here's the point. I have become increasingly convinced that in order to understand and appreciate Paul and the first-century Roman Empire one really should reread Acts in a cramped, damp sailboat, with no privacy, while the boat is pitching and heaving in a storm, packed with strangers, all of whom are pitching, and some of whom are heaving as well.

Because the context of the biblical story from Genesis to Acts is the Land, with its "great and howling wilderness," scorching deserts, sharp valleys, and craggy mountains, it is incredibly beneficial to spend time in those areas in order to understand and appreciate the physical context of Scripture and the people who were shaped culturally and religiously by that environment. However, with Jesus' utilization of boats on the Sea of Galilee in his ministry, the stage of the biblical drama begins to shift from solid to liquid.

Acts completes the shift of the story from land to sea. Acts is a book of action and actors on the dynamic stage of the Mediterranean world of the first century. Paul has the leading role in this drama but the cast includes other apostles and other missionaries as well as Roman officials, seafaring pagans, Jewish and Greek antagonists, and Jewish and Greek believers in Paul's message. Paul's actions and reactions, his suffering and his success, can best be imagined and appreciated from within the volatile, passionate, glorious, and polyglot world in which he traveled and experimented with the good news of the kingdom of God. We learn to understand Paul and his writings more realistically if we can repeat some of his actions in their original location. In doing so, we may discover that at times Paul's actions speak louder than his words and that his words then take on fresh relevancy.

In Scripture, indeed among sacred texts of any kind, Acts is unique. Acts is probably the only ancient sacred text that provides adequate information for voyage planning. It is, I discovered, one of the best descriptive documents in existence of sailing in the Mediterranean during the first century. Unlike Homer's *Odyssey*, real ports, thirty-seven in all, are named in Acts. The conditions of weather and descriptions of sailing are precise. Names and dates match the archeological and historical evidence.[3] Acts is a useful text, not only for preparing a sermon, but for planning a voyage on the Mediterranean.

The sea is far less susceptible to visible alterations by human intervention than the land. Human activity on land transforms the footpaths and villages of biblical times to superhighways and urban sprawl today, making physical and emotional connections to the past difficult for the traveler. Not so with the sea. Weather patterns have not changed significantly from the time of Acts. The summer gales, the powerful *meltemi* depicted in Acts, still blow from the northwest. The winter storms still begin in November. The descendants of the Greeks, of Philippians, of Ephesians, of Corinthians, and of the Macedonians whom Paul met, still inhabit the islands and port cities. Sailing yachts, colorful little fishing boats, and island ferries continue to tie up in harbors used by Jason, Odysseus, and Paul. Above those ancient harbors, pagan temples, albeit largely in ruins today, are still visible from the sea.

Since the classic *St. Paul the Traveler and Roman Citizen* by William Ramsey was first published in 1895, or Roland Allen's *Missionary Methods: St. Paul's or Ours?* first appeared in 1912, excellent research has produced an additional abundance of rich insights into the social, political, economic, and religious environment of Acts that help modern Bible readers to understand the first-century world in which Paul moved. My goal during the sabbatical and since is to build on the extensive research by providing what is usually missing—a sea level perspective on Paul, a view of the archeological sites by their ancient approaches from the seaports,

---

3. For an investigation of the accuracy of the details mentioned in Acts, White's book *Evidence,* is a fine introduction.

insights from the challenging experiences of sea travel, and perspectives on Paul from encounters with people living in the ports visited by Paul.

These perspectives are informative and applicable to the faithful and relevant missionary task of western Christians in the context of globalization for the following reasons:

The World Is Like the Sea

The entire technologically-connected world in the twenty-first century, like the Mediterranean-connected Roman Empire of the first century, resembles the sea. In both the Roman Empire connected by the Mediterranean Sea and the current globalization connected by digital technology, the creative, energetic, and cooperating systems of human diversity generate both expectations and resentment simultaneously, creating the conditions for sudden, unforeseen, and sometimes deadly economic, social, religious, and political storms.

Our world, like the Roman Empire, like the sea itself, is unpredictable, unstable, changeable, and simultaneously beautiful and deadly. Like the sea, our world is full of potential and peril, is so promising, so disappointing. We can learn from Paul about this world, for he was a man of the Mediterranean Sea and a citizen of the Roman Empire.

The Church Is like a Ship at Sea

A Mediterranean cargo ship on a successful voyage is at once at home on the untamed sea while not being overcome, overwhelmed, or controlled by it. The first-century church, especially congregations located in the port cities of the empire, resembled a ship on a promising, high-risk voyage toward the vision of the kingdom of God. This ship-church was at home in the dangerous empire, utilizing its power while avoiding being controlled by it. The motley collection of humanity attracted to the early congregations resembled the passengers aboard first-century ships, united in commitment despite the risks, cooperating in order to reach a common goal, and utilizing the power of the untamed winds to make progress by constantly adjusting the sails and the ship's heading.

The twenty-first-century church, insofar as it is a movement of the kingdom of God, is, or has the potential to again become, like a ship at sea. We can learn from Paul about the ship-like church, for he was at home both on Mediterranean cargo ships and in the churches located in the port cities of the Mediterranean.

Living by Faith Is like Sailing

As the disciples discovered on the Sea of Galilee, and as Paul demonstrates so clearly in his post-conversion life voyage on the Mediterranean Sea, to follow Jesus both literally and figuratively involved sailing. For both sailing on the sea and living by faith, life is constantly unstable. It is a ceaseless balance between capsize and progress, exhilaration and alarm, ballast and sail. Constant adjustments in direction are necessary in order to at once utilize the power of the wind and avoid being capsized by it. Sailing and following Jesus are both risky endeavors. But for as long as the voyage lasts, this life is one of abundance of both rewards and suffering.

We can learn from Paul who, in following Jesus' high-risk call to represent the kingdom of God in the Roman Empire, learned to survive and navigate both the Mediterranean Sea and the pagan culture of the empire. His letters to the churches he established are survival and navigational instructions for the ship-like church in the sea-like empire.

What follows are perspectives from the Mediterranean Sea on empire, church, and the life of faith, but especially on Paul and his sea-shaped view of the Roman Empire and vision of the kingdom of God. Paul and his perspectives have implications for Western Christians for we Western Christians live in the "uttermost parts of the world" to which Jesus sent Paul. We have sought to make ourselves at home there. Achieving that, we have confused our home with the Promised Land, and have yielded to the temptation to protect our territory, to control our society, and most of all, to be safe and secure.

But we "must go down to the sea again, to the lonely sea and sky." For what we need "is a tall ship and a star to steer her by."[4]

Linford Stutzman, aboard *SailingActs*, Finike, Turkey

4. Slightly adapted from the opening lines of "Sea Fever" by John Masefield.

Acknowledgments

WRITING A BOOK IS like sailing. You can claim to do it single-handedly, but many others who are not actually on the boat are on board in other ways, making the voyage a success. These are the ones who give support, direction, and encouragement. They pass on valuable advice from their own journeys. They warn of hidden dangers and navigational careless-ness from their own experience and expertise. I want to thank several key groups of people and individuals who did this so well:

The discussion group of Zion Mennonite Church near Portland, Oregon, who over a period of months read through the first draft of the manuscript and gave valuable feedback from their perspective as people committed to peace, justice, and being relevant and effective witnesses in an alienated and disillusioned world.

The Eastern Mennonite University students of mission, who were given the second manuscript as a course reading requirement with the assignment to critique and evaluate the ideas and conclusions. They did so from their perspective as young adults facing a globalized and uncertain future, with a commitment to Jesus and the kingdom as well as doubt and questions about the ability of the church in the West to be relevant in their future.

The graduate students around the world taking the online course I taught for Eastern Mennonite Seminary, "The Church in Mission." Again reading and evaluating the manuscript as part of their course assign-ments, they discussed with me and with each other their perspectives on the manuscript, globalization, and the perceptions of the United States from their locations in Israel, Palestine, Columbia, and Nicaragua, as well as from several places within the United States.

David Stutzman, graduate student at Fuller Theological Seminary in the School of International Studies, researched the background, checked accuracy, and identified places for strengthening the manuscript as part of his directed study on Paul and empire. His insight, both as a student and son, was uniquely objective and subjective. I am especially grateful for this opportunity to learn, like Paul often did, from someone so close who has shared so much of my life's journey of faith in the world.

Jon Stutzman, who as both professional actor and son taught me almost everything I know about stages, scripts, drama, and acting, and how these reflect and connect with the drama of human history and divine action.

Janet Stutzman, co-captain on *SailingActs* and the journey of faith, as well as first mate in every sense of the word.

Thank you.

List of Figures

part 1

The World Is Like the Sea

I SAW THE OCEAN for the first time when I was five years old. Although our family lived about a two-hour drive from Newport, Oregon, my father, whose income from logging and farming kept the family clothed and fed, and who also pastored a small church in our community of Cascadia, seldom had time for a vacation. But somehow on that unforgettable day Dad had squeezed, not only a day in at the coast, but also his family of seven into our 1950 Ford sedan.

I stared in astonishment and a little alarm out at across the vast Pacific Ocean. I could not see the other side! "Where does it end?" I asked.

"It doesn't really," Dad replied, "but if you went far enough on the ocean you would reach Japan or anywhere else in the world."

I tried to imagine Japan across the endless water and, failing that, settled for wading in the waves along the beach. But from that moment on I dreamed of crossing that ocean one day, all the way to Japan.

The waves on the Oregon coast can be glorious and terrifying as they smash, roaring and foaming, into the rugged rocks that make the Oregon coast so picturesque. "Where do they come from?" I asked.

"From storms far away," Dad answered.

For years after that encounter with the sea, whenever gale winds caused the tall fir trees to sway and dance outside of our house in the Cascade foothills, I imagined them to be the tall masts of sailing ships in storms at sea.

I have never sailed to Japan or experienced a storm on a boat in the Pacific, but the Mediterranean, as the myriad of ancient shipwrecks attest, has lured and destroyed the lives of many daring, foolhardy, desperate soldiers, sailors, traders, and slaves. It lured me too.

For most of my life since viewing the ocean in Oregon, I have lived and travelled on the other side of America's oceans. I have been awed by the beauty of human achievements throughout history, the power of ancient and contemporary culture, and the deadly storms that destroy civilizations.

The world is like the sea, and Paul, growing up in Tarsus, a port city on the eastern end of the Mediterranean, was a man of the sea.

1

Empires: The Quest for Stability

Empires

EVERYWHERE WE SAIL AROUND the Mediterranean, the remains of ancient empires are visible, at least in those places where modern empire building has not buried the amazingly durable remains of the past under parking lots, shopping malls, gigantic resorts, office buildings, and apartment complexes. At the edge of ancient harbors, magnificent temples crumble into piles of half-buried, eroded stone next to busy streets, boutiques, and sidewalk cafes. Many theaters, once the scene of Greek comedies, are overgrown, garbage-strewn tragedies.

If the Mediterranean is the cradle of civilization, it is also the graveyard of empires. The overgrown archeological sites are the neglected cemeteries of past human attempts to control the future, to live securely, to dominate the environment and their enemies. The ruined temples and theaters are the sad, magnificent headstones of once impressive, but always partial and flawed achievements of human creativity and control that have long been laid to rest. The descendants of these empires continue to live in the areas of former greatness. The inhabitants of the Roman Empire, once united by the Mediterranean Sea, are now divided into nations with different languages, religions, cultures, and aspirations.

While the attraction to empire building in some form or another seems to be universal, not all civilizations are equally successful in establishing vast empires, nor are all regions of the planet favorable to sustaining them. The majority of societies must settle for tribal, local, and perhaps national control. However, the *quest* for control and stability on all levels of human relational organization seems to be universal. Egypt of ancient times and Rome of the first century were two of the most successful in recorded Mediterranean history.

Egypt's achievements are legendary. While there is no evidence that Saul[1] had ever visited Egypt, many thousands of other Jews were living and flourishing in the port city of Alexandria during his lifetime in the first century. Because of the relative ease of travel by ship between Alexandria and the seaports of Palestine, stories of the marvels of Egypt—two of the Seven Wonders of the Ancient World were in Egypt—would have circulated throughout the Mediterranean, including to Jerusalem, impressing Saul and everyone else. Anyone who has viewed the Great Pyramid of Giza, built almost 5,000 years ago and towering above the desert landscape by more than 146 meters, understands why, for this incredible structure held the record of being the tallest human construction in the world for over 4,000 years. The nearly eight million visitors who come to Egypt every year continue to be impressed.

I remember one particular group of thirty Eastern Mennonite University students on the Middle East cross-cultural study semester visiting, on the day after we arrived from the USA, the pyramids of Giza, the oldest of the Seven Wonders, and the only one of these Wonders still substantially intact.

"I cannot believe they did this without cell-phones or computers!" "How could they organize that many workers?" "Why would they spend years and fortunes building a tomb?" they asked with jet-lagged awe, astonishment, and disbelief.

These awe-inspiring pyramids are massive monuments to the ideals of empire—durability, stability, dominance, power, and control. To this day the pyramids testify to Egypt's successes in achieving their ideals

---

1. I will use the names "Saul" and "Paul" following the usage in Acts. This will help differentiate between the developments and transitions that began before and occurred after the encounter with Jesus on the Damascus road.

through human organization and exploitation of their natural and human resources. The shape of the pyramid mirrors the shape of the social structure of empire, a monument that demonstrates the staggering human cost of building and maintaining the power and glory of the empire carried out by the majority at the lower levels, and the vast rewards for the a small number of elite at the top. Why do empires exist? How do they emerge?

The explanatory foundations of the origins and continued existence of the Mediterranean empires, large and small, durable or fleeting, are linked to their creation myths that explain the nature of both the cosmos and the empire. The use of the term "myth" does not connote fabrication or an untrue story. Myth refers to the official, perhaps sacred story, the collective, selective memory of a people sharing some kind of common identity. These creation myths serve to explain and clarify the reasons for divine blessing and favor for a particular people and the ways that these blessings and divine assistance can be sustained. These stories legitimize the dominance of the favored groups of people and identify their enemies. Creation myths may justify conquest, slavery, pillage, and destruction. They often support the right of the emperor to rule and for defeated subjects to serve the empire. These myths are visible in the monuments, temples, statues, triumphal arches, mosaics, and *steles* around the Mediterranean. Creation myths help organize and sustain the power of the rulers in their personal and collective quest for lasting control of their part of the world. There are powerful advantages to empire building if the creator and sustainer of both the universe and the empire are believed to be the same god, and if the empire's subjects view their rulers as representing their powerful gods. A brief look at creation myths in relation to empire may be helpful.

Creation: Sea, Land, and the Quest for Stability

In the beginning was sea and chaos. On this both the Egyptian and the Hebrew creation stories agree, as do many other versions of creation myths around the world. The first creative acts of the god(s) bring order to this chaos, and life begins. Division between land and sea is one of the several acts early in the creation sequences, for this division is the condition for human life to exist.

But it is the Hebrew version that gives the most unique insights into and perspective on the universal human propensity for empire building. This biblical creation account shaped the worldview of the young Saul, his understanding of the Roman Empire, the kingdom of Israel, and eventually his vision of the kingdom of God. The biblical account also has vital prophetic implications for Western Christians.

It is not within the scope of this study to compare and contrast various creation stories, but rather to demonstrate the distinctive insights that the biblical story of creation and fall bring to empire building, that seemingly irresistible attraction throughout history of humans to build systems of control over nature, the future, and other people, including women and enemies. This attraction to create order out of chaos and stability through domination, depicted in the story of the fall, shapes human social relationships through every level of complexity, from the relationship between two people to complex global empires. In contrast to the creation stories of Egypt and other the ancient Mediterranean empires, the biblical creation story implies that all human empire building is associated with sin and separation from the Creator. In this regard, the biblical account of creation is unique among creation stories of empires.

How is the creation story anti-empire? We begin with the trees in the Garden of Eden. There were many good trees in the garden; in the very middle were two special ones—the Tree of Life and the Tree of Knowledge of Good and Evil (Gen 2:9). This is a significant pairing. One would expect that if God had provided a special, positive "Tree of Life" and invited the human pair to eat of it for eternal blessing, the forbidden tree would have been labeled the "Tree of Death." Or logically, if the forbidden tree was called the "Tree of Knowledge," that the opposite would have been the "Tree of Innocence" or the "Tree of Ignorance" in the story. However, the names of the trees are "Life" and "Knowledge of Good and Evil," which are not immediately recognizable as contrasting categories.

In addition, the Tree of Knowledge contains the knowledge of both good and evil, not just evil, as one would expect. What could possibly be wrong with knowing *good*? The contrasting categories of good and evil are contained in the one forbidden tree. The names of the trees in the story, while contradicting conventional wisdom, provide unexpected and profound insight into the shape of relationships in the history of human organization.

According to the story, Adam and Eve did not eat of the Tree of Life. Why would they want to? They were already alive. Nothing in the story indicates that death was present anywhere in their experience. They did not need more life and they were not familiar with or threatened by death. They could not be tempted by what they already had. So while the Tree of Life from which they could have eaten was present in the middle of the garden, it was the Tree of Knowledge of Good and Evil in which the serpent waited to point out their limitations and their potential.

We discover, as we look at the long view of history, that the serpent mostly told the truth. "You will not die," the serpent said to the woman and the man with her, "for God knows that when you eat of it your eyes will be opened, and you will be like God [or gods],[2] knowing good and evil" (Gen 3:4b–5). That this tree would give Adam and Eve the ability to know good and evil was, of course, correct. According to the serpent, they would then "become as gods," which was also partly true, and they would do so without any negative results. This last part was a complete lie, but not obviously so, depending on how death was understood in the humans' imagination. The temptation, therefore, included the denial of death, or at least the failure to acknowledge it.

According to the story, the relational change between Adam and Eve following the eating of the attractive fruit of the Tree of Knowledge of Good and Evil was immediate and dramatic. Their eyes were suddenly opened in a negative way to their gender differences, which they attempted to rectify by trying to cover themselves. Their relationship with God was replaced by fear, and when God finally tracked them down he found them cowering among the other trees in the Garden. Speaking in the story, God describes the immediate, permanent consequences present in human history ever since.

---

2. The Hebrew word used here is *elohim*, translated in English as either "God" or "gods" depending on the context. Here it is not clear and either translation has contextual validity.

Adam and Eve's options no longer include the abundant life of Eden for they are thrown out of the Garden. Return to the Garden and the Tree of Life is denied. In their autonomy, these humans would now be free to choose good and evil of which they now had knowledge. However, their choices for the options of either good or evil could not give them access to life. Death was inevitably to become a part of the human experience. Relationships between men and women, separated from the life-giving power of the Creator, would now be characterized by power, dependency, hierarchy, and exploitation. These relationships could be relatively good or evil, depending on human choices, but they would never be the same. The vanity, selfishness, competition, deceit, betrayal, and mutual exploitation that we see later in the relationships among the gods of Greece and Rome were the human experience at the beginning of history. Humans did indeed become as gods.

But something else has occurred beyond the personal. The harmony and stability within the Garden has been replaced by social competition, instability, contingency, and chaos. The social world of humans now resembled the sea. The human quest now was to re-create this lost stability and security by exercising power and control through the knowledge of good and evil. This quest is the condition for empire building.

The Shape of Human Empires

Human relationships, cultures, institutions, and history are all shaped by the universal human dichotomizing of life, people, actions, and experience into good and evil categories. Autonomous humans seek to bring order out of chaos, stability in unpredictable environments, to seek abundance and life, to avoid and delay death as long as possible. Because humans are aware that death is inevitable, the quest for increasing knowledge of good and evil in order to extend and enhance life (good) on one hand, and to avoid, dominate, or destroy all that threatens the quality or length of life (evil) on the other, is relentless. Cultural, ideological, religious, and even scientific systems provide the knowledge of what belongs in these two basic categories.

Power, derived from knowledge, leads to the stratification of all relationships within a society. Within all relationships in a society—whether within institutions, religions, or nations—individuals and groups with the authority to define good and evil for themselves and others are among the powerful. Powerful individuals form groups of elite who dominate others. Those with the ability to utilize and control the knowledge necessary to make decisions about good and evil have power over those who do not. With few exceptions, those with this power use it first for their own and their own people's life enhancement and extension, and against others who may threaten this pursuit. "Indeed, the whole organization of knowledge could be seen as a construction designed to control the world."[3]

In effective societies, the elite exercise and sustain their power by successfully convincing those less privileged that they will benefit immediately or ultimately by cooperating. The powerful may need to use coercion and violence to ensure acquiescence among those who reject the premises and promises of the powerful. The promises from the elite can be incredibly attractive, especially when these elite embody and demonstrate the success they promise. Voluntary slavery, such as that in ancient Egypt, with the masses of poor willingly helping to build the pyramids of the pharaohs with the belief that they would share the pharaoh's glory and life beyond death, is one historical example. More subtle forms, such as going into serious debt to purchase a status symbol like a luxury vacation home or a Hummer, are common today. We will return to the marketing empires and modern voluntary slavery later.

In order to simplify this complex and vast subject for university students I have developed several diagrams that will be introduced in this chapter and used in subsequent ones. These diagrams are only meant to provide conceptual tools for thinking about empire from the perspective of the biblical history of the people of faith in relation to empires. The history of the world, empire building, and the quest for stability is far more complex than these simple pictures can possibly represent. Yet, I believe that they accurately reflect alternative themes and prophetic perspectives on human history within the biblical narrative, including Paul's recorded actions, speeches, and letters. The following diagram, based on the biblical creation story, reflects the general social patterns that inevitably emerge as knowledge of good and evil is exercised as unequal power within all relationships and human organizations and systems.

3. Murray, "Introduction," xvii.

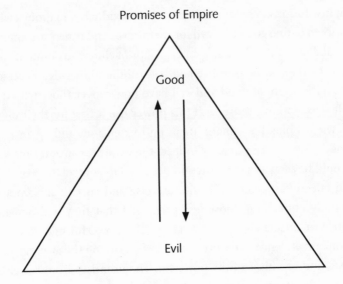

FIGURE 1.1. Empire Shaped by the Exercise
of Knowledge of Good and Evil in Human Society

The social dynamics of power to control knowledge and the shape of human society and relationships where control is achieved can be seen above. The ability to define good and evil for others gives relative power over others within any human relationship or organization. One's success in achieving good within the framework of these definitions raises the status of the individual and increases their power relative to those who are unsuccessful in achieving the good, or who chose evil instead. The higher one rises toward the good of the system, the greater the rewards and the fiercer the competition. This ensures that relatively few achieve the pinnacle of success. Most individuals however, strive to achieve the status and the corresponding rewards of the top position, seeking, at the very least, to identify with and emulate those who have achieved high levels of power, success, and status.

All religions, ancient and modern, polytheistic, monotheistic, or non-theistic, tribal or universal, utilize some form of good/evil categorization to organize life. Behavior, beliefs, and material objects fall into the good and evil religious categories and may be given labels such as "right/ wrong," "clean/unclean," "spiritual/carnal," and "enlightened/unenlightened." The lists of dichotomy in religions are creative, endless, and contradictory among religions. All religions promise some form of the good life, variously characterized as wealthy, healthy, beautiful, secure, blessed, happy, honorable, true, abundant, or fulfilling. All religions promise some form of eternal life.[4] Within all religions, the negative consequences—some form of death resulting from what the religion defines as evil—are motivators.

Within all organized human institutions, including religions, individuals and movements emerge that take counterpositions to the official doctrine. These counterpositions challenge and threaten the orthodox positions, question the traditions and the interpretation of the leaders, and resist the inevitable abuses of power of those in positions of authority. These resistance movements and the people who represent them may be especially attractive to those suffering from the burdens placed on them by those in authority.

Where religion is wedded to the empire, religious renewal and political revolution are often inseparable. Karl Marx was only partly right when he observed that religion is "the opiate of the people," whose suffering at the hands of the powerful elite is somewhat alleviated by their faith in eternal reward. Other Marxist theoreticians, such as Antonio Gramsci, have pointed out the opposite role religion can take—that of liberation and revolution.[5] Those who challenge the status quo may be labeled as heretics, excluded, and even persecuted as evil. If their influence begins to severely threaten the status of the authorities, they may even be executed.

Secular ideologies function in ways similar to religion, attracting adherents around themes and promises of individual and collective power and material reward. Ideologies, like religions, make promises for life improvement. Like religions, they ground their doctrine on creation stories, albeit naturalistic, scientific versions. Like religions, secular ideologies dichotomize between good and evil, effective or ineffective, revolutionary or reactive, capitalist or socialist, liberal or conservative, Republican or Democrat. They may utilize religious language—"those not for us are

---

4. Although in some definitions, for instance within Buddhism, eternal life is not conceptualized as existence that is experienced by self-conscious individuals.

5. My dissertation, *Gramsci's Theory*, contains a full discussion of these Marxist viewpoints. See pp. 34–39.

against us"— in their motivational speeches. They persecute and, in extreme cases, even kill the ideological heretics who may threaten the success of the ideology or the stability and security of the system.

The biblical story of creation and fall identifies the patterns of domination and subordination that shape the human organization of empire as either sin or the results of sin. While often overlooked, this is an incredibly revolutionary perspective on so much of what is deemed to be good in human history. The good promises of abundance, security, happiness, freedom, power, and glory, which are more or less realized within every system, are ultimately and inherently flawed and false. While there are relatively good and evil systems of relationships, societies, and empires, all of these operate within a closed system that ends in death. None of the systems of dichotomy and control can give life. Life is from the Creator only. "Sometimes there is a way that seems to be right, but in the end it is the way to death" (Prov 16:25). Thus, the roads in human empires really do not ultimately lead to the promised rewards, or even merely to Rome. They all lead to death.

The story of the fall is the story of the human condition throughout history. It would perhaps be more accurate to understand the fall not only as the "original sin" but also as the permanent, universal sin inherent in every human relationship and institution of society, attracting every individual with the promise of stability in the face of chaos, confidence when facing an uncertain future, security in a dangerous world, a good life instead of suffering and death. This permanent and universal temptation, like death itself, is not only just quite common, it is inevitable. As the young Saul learned this creation story, his understanding of the Roman Empire in which he was growing up was being shaped.

The Exodus Movement out of Empire

The world view of the young Saul growing up in Tarsus was also shaped by a second story about the nature of empire, the exodus, an event celebrated annually by every Jew in the Roman Empire no matter where they lived. The Passover ritual had deep implications for Saul in Tarsus, as it did for all of the Jewish communities scattered throughout the empire, from those living in occupied Jerusalem to those residing in Rome itself.

As the Jews in the Roman Empire told themselves the Passover story of liberation at the hand of Moses, leading their ancestors out of the slavery of Egypt through the wilderness toward the Promised Land, they were reminded of the destructive patterns of the empire in which they lived. At the same time, they were reminded of the promises of God that offered liberation and life to their ancestors in Egypt.

We look again at the pyramid-shaped Egyptian Empire. The pharaoh was not "*as* a god, *knowing* good and evil" but, in the official and popular view, *was* a god, defining good and evil. In the story of the exodus, good and evil are also defined, but in a completely contrasting way. Good and evil are defined by the direction of the movement either toward or away from the promise of life in the land as demonstrated below.

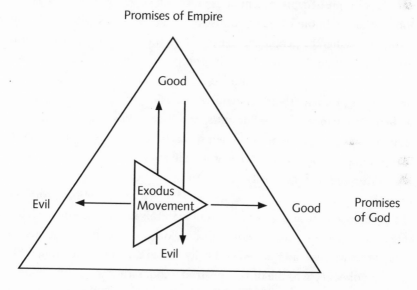

FIGURE 1.2. The Dynamics of the Exodus Movement

The power of the movement is the promise of life. It is liberating. The movement threatens the empire because it refuses to play by the self-serving order of the empire's ruling elite. The contrasting promises shape contradictory perceptions of reality, as well as the actions among the people who believe them. The exodus movement competes with the static "divine" order of Egypt, as well as with that of other small nations of the regions through which it passes. It threatens those with the power to define and enforce the empire's good for their own benefit. It gives immediate and relevant hope to those who are designated as evil in the empire and suffer because of it. The movement cuts across the cultural patterns of empire, causing consternation or celebration depending on the social position of those within the empires through which the movement occurs.

The distinct features of the movement are shaped by the promises of a new, secure home. The journey toward that promise, however, is marked by vulnerability, insecurity, and change. The reality of the promise is demonstrated by the actions of those on the journey who believe in the promises. The exodus is a movement of faith, a prophetic parade toward God's promises performed in and among empires.

The power of Moses was linked to his leadership toward the promise. He relinquished his potential position of power in pharaoh's court and instead embodied God's promises among the slaves with whom he identified. When the people looked at Moses, they saw potential freedom, the Land of Promise, and life itself. The people experienced the power of God in their deliverance, both from Egypt and from their enemies en route to the promise. Their deliverance from Egyptian tyranny, their subsequent sustenance in the wilderness, and their victories in invading the land inhabited by others were all demonstrations to the Israelites and the surrounding nations of God's power to deliver on promises.

Moses led with authority, not from the top of a human system, but from the front of the exodus movement. He demonstrated the promises of God by his faith, and served the people in this liberating, empowering role. It was through Moses' own faith developed in his close relationship to God that Moses commanded authority. It was a tenuous and vulnerable position; obedience to the directions from God, rather than enforcement of his own decisions sustained Moses' authority. Moses organized the people not in the familiar hierarchical division of status and labor, but horizontally, an organized mobilization for travel, a long journey of faith toward the promise.

The structure of the newly emerging Hebrew society was shaped by the vision of and orientation toward the promise. It was shaped by the blessing of God's presence, as well as by the resistance and hardships encountered along the way. This shape is in contrast to the hierarchical, pyramid-like structure of empires organized for stability, defense, domination, and endurance. The shape of the movement of Israel in the wilderness is for mobility and invasion.

The shape of this movement did not provide the usual stability and predictability promised by kings to their subjects; rather it was geared for unstable, unpredictable progress, toward fulfillment of an unseen promise, and for cutting across the familiar and powerful good/evil patterns of society. From the diagram it can be noted that if the forward movement were to cease, the effect would be a rotation. The movement would become a small pyramid with its point oriented upwards towards the good of empire, rather than towards God's promises. Like a bicycle, stability is contingent upon momentum. Momentum requires continuous power. The same is true for the exodus movement. It was dynamic, sustained through the power of hope and faith in God and God's promises. It was vulnerable, utterly dependant on God for survival. The movement was extremely difficult and uncomfortable. The patterns of good and evil in society may not give life, but they make it orderly, and order, in the short run, is preferable to insecurity, chaos, vulnerability, and unpredictability. These are the conditions of the wilderness.

The exodus movement continues after Moses' death. The judges, those prophetic leaders of the conquest, led the movement not from the top but from the front as Moses had, exercising the power of God that Moses had demonstrated. While the subject of the violence of the conquest normally gets the attention, it is the contingency, the disorganized, spontaneous, and inherently vulnerable ways the battles transpired, that is unique in the history of successful warfare.

It could be noted here that the maps in the back of Bibles that depict movement, those colorful trails on the maps left behind by Abraham and Sarah and their extended family as they wandered toward the promise, or behind Moses and the children of Israel as they moved in the direction of the promise through the wilderness, these maps of movement represent the high points of faith. The maps that show tribal territories, diagrams of the temple, maps that depict stability, permanence, and static structure, are snapshots of the movement's capitulation to the original and permanent temptation of humanity to organize for security and build stability and control. They are pictures of immanent decline and eventual defeat. This brings us to the kingdom in the Promised Land.

The Kingdom—Like Other Nations

The third primary story that shaped the young Saul's view of the world and his place in it was the biblical story of his ancestors living in the Promised Land. This story includes the invasion of Joshua's rag-tag "army," and continues to the rise and fall of the kingdoms of Judah and Israel. Let us examine the way this story contributes to Saul's understanding of the movement of Jesus before and after he met him on the Damascus road.

For the invaders of the exodus, living in an alternative, vulnerable, contingent movement had its disadvantages. The dependency on God made the outcome of every battle unpredictable, not because of God's capriciousness, but because of human sin and loss of faith. The appeal to "be like other nations" needs to be understood as a form of the temptation in the Garden of Eden, of being in autonomous and calculated control of one's destiny. What transpired is one of the classic temptation sagas in the Bible. The story of the people of Israel liberated from an incredibly successful, durable empire of Egypt is also the story of seeking to replicate, under the God of the exodus, the stability, predictability, and security of the Egypt they had left behind and to which they could not return. The judges, while effectively leading the Hebrews to victory, were not kings. Their leadership was temporary and rural. They could not make the same kinds of promises that the kings of Egypt made to their people.

Israel's desire for a king was a temptation to have a leader who could take them into the direction of stability, control, collective power, and lasting glory, just like the nations that threatened or defeated them. The dependency on God and God's judges was problematic and limiting. Israel wanted to compete with the other nations on their own terms. But this experiment with kings, with only brief exceptions, was a dismal failure.[6]

The slaves had been delivered from the most powerful empire of the time through the prophetic intervention of Moses acting in the power of God. The invasion and subduing of the residents of the land they had been promised was originally contingent upon a relationship of trust and obedience to the God who alone could save them. This contingency of

---

6. For the discussion of the temptation of the people of Israel to build an empire like other nations, Bright's *The Kingdom of God* is a classic.

obedience, imperative to the victory on the battlefield, made the Israelites vulnerable. Would any other people have responded differently?

A review of the sad history under the kings, the division of the kingdom, the dismal succession of evil kings, and the defeats and eventual captivity of the remaining small kingdom of Judah is unnecessary, for it is well known. While prophets like Isaiah and Jeremiah pointed to both the vision of a kingdom of righteousness and peace and the failure of the kings to rule with either, the desire to be like other nations prevailed. Not only did Israel experience some of the stability and status like other kingdoms around them under kings David and Solomon, and occasional short victories and relative autonomy under other leaders, Israel also experienced defeat and humiliation, just like other small, local empires. Israel did indeed become, not only like other nations in general, but in some ways like Egypt on a smaller scale, as the figure below depicts.

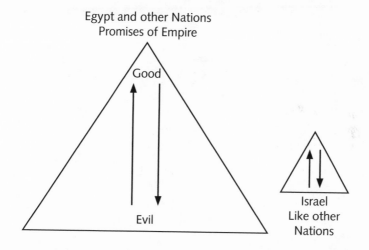

FIGURE 1.3. The Kingdom of Israel: From Movement to Stability

Throughout history the predictable and dreary story of empires is repeated. It is not history that is repeating itself, but humans repeating history, persistently attempting, through the knowledge of good and evil, to achieve stability in a world that resembles the sea. Israel was no different. They wanted to be like the other nations in spite of their awareness that they were God's special people. However, Israel matched neither the durable power of Egypt from which they came nor the amazing success of the Roman Empire of the first century.

By the first century, it was the Roman Empire that had occupied and subjugated the peoples around the Mediterranean Sea, including the supposedly blessed and God-protected people of Israel. The power of Rome was felt and the promises of Rome were seen everywhere around the rim of the entire Mediterranean Sea. The Mediterranean, the liquid, pagan heart of the empire, made it possible for Rome to exercise its power and to demonstrate its promises to all of the inhabitants around its rim, including Palestine. Because of this, the Mediterranean Sea also brought Rome's peril to those people it had brought under its control, including the former kingdoms of Israel and Judah. The Romans had gone to sea, and the seaport of Tarsus, Saul's boyhood home, was immersed in the pagan world of the Roman Sea.

2

The Power, Promises, and Perils of the Pagan Sea

Power and Control on Display

SAUL'S HOMETOWN, TARSUS, IS a seaport on the Mediterranean. Living in Tarsus gave the young Saul, attending Jewish schools, an early awareness of the contrasts of the power and promises of the Roman Empire with the power and promises of God in his own people's traditions.

The Mediterranean Sea was the liquid, pagan center of the Roman Empire. It was the domination and utilization of this sea that enabled Rome to subdue the variety of powerful ethnic groups around the entire rim of the Mediterranean, to consolidate their vast resources, and redirect the longings of these individuals and groups toward the enhancement of Rome's self-interest. This was a remarkable achievement. Rome demonstrated that by utilizing the sea and eliminating anyone else who tried to do the same, their control of the people and resources around the Mediterranean could grow without limit. World empires would later seek to emulate this vision of limitless expansion on vastly larger seas.

The political power and economic promises of Rome road the waves of the sea, not only to seaports like Tarsus, but all the way to Jerusalem in the Land of Promise. Herod the Great ruled Palestine under Rome from 37 to 4 BC and during that time he sought to ensure that he would be remembered forever, for he was one of the world's great builders. Throughout Palestine the trademark gigantic and beautifully cut stones of Herod's buildings can still be seen in the ruins or part of existing structures of tombs, temples, cities, palaces, and fortresses.

I have never ceased to be impressed by Herod and his eternal palaces, fortresses, and complete cities. Year after year these sites continue to attract hurrying tourists and methodical scholars, for in the most unlikely places, on mountain tops, in inhospitable deserts, on sandy beaches, and sites far below sea level, any place where it was difficult to build it seems, where fresh water was scarce and the topography challenging, there Herod built. The palaces and fortresses such as the Heroduim near Bethlehem, Masada, and Machaerus[1] overlooking the Dead Sea, the palace at the winter resort of Jericho, these places of conspicuous opulence and luxury in the wilderness declared Herod's—and Rome's—domination of the land. Herod's selection of building sites was designed to flaunt the power and permanence, not only of Rome over the people of Palestine, but over nature itself. Long before the invention of the pumps and pipes necessary for pressurized water systems, slaves toiled each and every day, staggering up and down the rocky cliff paths of the Herodium and Masada with jars of water to empty into the cavernous cisterns. The cisterns needed to be constantly full so that on a moment's notice Herod and any of his many important visitors could drop by and cavort in the swimming pools with their magnificent views overlooking their arid desert surroundings.

Rome's domination of the sea was also on display in the thoroughly pagan city of Caesarea Maritima, built on Palestine's sandy beach. There Herod had built a harbor, completely artificial. The underwater concrete remains poured two thousand years ago can still be seen.[2] Herod's palace, built out into the sea itself, and the theater facing west toward Rome across the waves, all were designed to prove to the Jews of Palestine that Rome

---

1. Machaerus, in present-day Jordan, represents the stark contrast between the dominance of Rome displayed in Palestine by Herod the Great and the vulnerability of those anticipating the coming kingdom of God demonstrated by John the Baptist. The traditional region of John the Baptist's ministry is within view of Machaerus.

2. The article "Caesarea Maritima" by Hohenfelder, published in the February 1987 issue of *National Geographic*, gives a graphic overview of Herod's magnificent achievement of both connecting Palestine to Rome and bringing Rome to Palestine.

could re-create the world in its own image. Rome ruled the Mediterranean Sea, and because of that, the Mediterranean world.

Herod brought the reality of this triumph of Rome's empire to the land where the power and glory of Israel's past kings and God's promises were faded memories of the past or remote, far-fetched dreams of the future. Rome ruled in the present and by all indications the future belonged to Rome as well.

In the first century, the triumph of Rome on permanent display around the rim of the Mediterranean, enticed and motivated the poor towards cooperation and voluntary enslavement. Patron/client relationships were an avenue for both exploitation and status enhancement and, as Bruce Malina notes, "permeated the whole of ancient Mediterranean society." Herod the Great was an example of privilege within the system of patron/client relationships that ensured cooperation of the upwardly mobile. Herod "was a client king of his patron, Caesar Augustus. The Capernaum centurion was a patron who sent word to Jesus through some 'friends,' a Roman name for client (Luke 7:6).... The title 'friend of Caesar' (John 19:12) was an official acknowledgment of imperial clientage."[3]

In the system of patronage "there was not the faintest trace of social equality, whether before the law or even in some ideal equality of all males. Institutionalized relationships between persons of unequal power statuses and resources were and are highly exploitative in nature. The 'best' families exerted power, applied vertically as force in harsh and impersonal fashion. People of higher status sought to maximize their gains without a thought to the losses of those with whom they interacted."[4]

The privileged elite comprised a very small minority of the population while possessing and controlling the vast majority of the empire's wealth. Only "two percent of the population in these societies belonged to the ruling elite, while about eight percent comprised the so-called service class in and around the cities. The remaining ninety percent lived in villages and worked on the land to support the first two classes.... Poverty was ... seen as the result of 'status-depriving' circumstances such as illness, debt, famine, or the death of a spouse (in the case of widows)."[5]

3. Malina, "Daily Life," 365.

4. Ibid., 364–65.

5. Joubert, "Reciprocity," 372.

While the way to achieve privilege in the Roman Empire may be somewhat different today, the ratio of wealthy elite to the working poor has changed little from the time of the Roman Empire. Neither has the nature of the pagan promises changed through the years. These attractive promises, embodied and often flaunted by the wealthy elite, serve to motivate the non-elite majority to strive upwards in order to achieve at least some of the rewards dangling above them, and to orient their lives toward the good defined by the rich and famous.

Today, in many of the same places where Herod constructed his palaces, fortresses, and cities to showcase his own and Rome's domination of land and sea, luxury hotels, islands of opulence surrounded by the harsh desert, salt water, and grinding poverty, function in similar ways. The elite of contemporary global empires sip cocktails, relax by sparkling freshwater swimming pools, enjoy massages, and are entertained each evening by floor shows, banquets, and gambling.

This was almost painfully apparent several years ago when my wife and I celebrated a wedding anniversary. We were wintering in Ashkelon, Israel, on *SailingActs* and decided to take a break from the writing I had been doing within its confining, rocking space. On the recommendation of some friends we had decided on the Mövenpick Resort Hotel on the eastern shore of the Dead Sea in Jordan, made possible due to a generous gift of two night's accommodation by friends in the area. This five-star resort is located in the area of Machaerus, one of Herod's desert palaces, where, tradition has it, the daughter of Herodias danced and John the Baptist was beheaded.

The taxi ride from the border crossing to the hotel took us south along the east bank of the Jordan River through a region of greenhouses, tractors, donkeys, then Bedouin tents, flocks of goats, and signs of poverty, through the barren moonscape surrounding the Dead Sea. Suddenly we arrived at the palm-lined grand entrance of the Mövenpick surrounded by manicured lawns. Smartly dressed and eager staff reached for our battered luggage. From our balcony off of our grand, luxurious room, we could see a Bedouin tent and a young boy tending a flock of sheep and goats. For the next two days we swam in the sparkling pools, read, ate fabulous meals, and basked in the sun, wallowing in wealth, beauty, and luxury served by staff people who quietly attended to our every need.

We were enjoying the benefits of globalization, the twenty-first-century equivalent of the Romanization of the Mediterranean. As in the first century, this island of abundance surrounded by poverty is a powerful enticement toward the top for those who have little. It seems that the world has not changed very much for either the citizens of powerful, wealthy empires or for the less fortunate, largely unnoticed poor who serve them, and us.

The Promises and Perils of the Pagan Sea

The promises of personal power and glory, potentially available for all who believe the compelling evidence that surrounds them and who strive to attain the rewards achieved by others within the system, are powerful. We'll examine the power of the pagan promises promoted around the rim of the Mediterranean by the elites of the Roman Empire, which worked so well for so long.

The gods of the empire exhibit the empire's promises, which the elite at the top of the pyramid embody and offer. Who can distinguish, when looking at the ageless statues discovered around the rim of the Mediterranean, between the power and glory of the gods and that of the emperors who made the power and the glory of the unseen gods visible and present, attractive and threatening, in the empire? The statues of gods and emperors look so similar. Today, even with important appendages missing and facial features eroded with the passage of time, they command attention, respect, and admiration, as well as a touch of fear. The gods' power, beauty, and attraction on one hand, and latent threat of their violence on the other, were emulated by the emperors. The power and the glory of the invisible gods were made visible in the power and glory of the emperors, their images, and their empire. Indeed, so indistinguishable was the emperor from the gods, that to worship the gods was a form of loyalty to the emperor.

The shape of society within the Roman Empire was that of a pyramid as depicted in the previous chapter. At the very top was the emperor, with less than 10 percent of the population directly connected to and sharing the power and status of the ruling elite. The rest of the population formed the economic base of the system. People on the top, the senators, equestrians, and other "respectable populace" such as wealthy landowners, set the agenda for everyone else. [6] What made the power of the elite minority at the top effective in keeping the poor majority engaged in maintaining a system of privilege they themselves would never enjoy?

Malina writes: "In the first century, the Roman elite formed a power syndicate with a network reaching out to elites in other cities of the region. These elites held a near monopoly of violence and therefore on social control throughout the empire. The Roman elite had control over the levers of political, political economic and political religious power." Malina notes that the ruling elite organized and consolidated their power "like the Mafia . . . ancient Roman elites and their co-opted non-Roman aristocrats were the center of dominant society. In both cases social control was based on fear, but also on a very broad consensus." [7]

The gods, whether real or imagined, and the permanent, universal temptation of humans desiring to be like the gods, to share in their power, domination, and control through the knowledge of good and evil, was the glue of the empire. The kingdoms of this world were, and still are, ruled by those who understand how to use the good and evil of popular gods for their personal and national accumulation of power and domination. The emperors of Rome were especially adept at making promises and sharing just enough of their accumulation of power and status with those who produced it to keep them hopeful and motivated. They knew how to deny power and status to those who refused to cooperate, and to threaten those who resisted their efforts of control with violence and death. Theses twin tools of control, desire and fear, good and evil if you will, were linked to the gods and exercised by emperors in the Roman Empire. [8]

"Power personified in the emperor or a god, reified in the central imperial city and its institutions, held full attention." [9] The cities, temples, and public buildings mirrored the social stratification that was perme-

---

6. Jeffers in provides a concise description of the privilege and status of class and wealth in the Roman Empire. See the pyramid-shaped diagram of social class in his *Greco-Roman World*, 181.

7. Malina, "Daily Life," 363.

8. The way that power was sustained in the empire through rituals in cities, imperial cult celebrations, and a host of other ways within the Roman Empire is described by Price, "Rituals and Power," 47–71.

9. Malina, "Daily Life," 360.

ated with pagan promises for compliance and threats against resistance. Economics, religion, and politics were unified in a system of control. "In the monarchic city-territories of the eastern Mediterranean, temples were political buildings, temple sacrifices were for the public good; the deity of the temple had a staff similar to the one a monarch had in the palace."[10] In the Roman Empire, as in all of the ancient empires around the Mediterranean, "certain things had to be in position." Among other things, "social obedience based on strict religious beliefs, and a royal dynasty based on divine right," kept the order intact.[11]

The world of Rome was shaped by inequality of power and social stratification continuously reinforced in public. Besides the temples, all public monuments, forums, palaces, streets, and harbors were showcases, not only of the power and glory of Rome and the status of the elite, but of the relative powerlessness and humility of the majority. The structure of power was built into the plans of the cities. While the elite enjoyed the luxury of their villas, the majority of the population lived in semi-squalor. The public spaces of the cities provided a way for the poorer majority to sample the luxury of the wealthy elite, for these spaces resembled the private houses of the wealthy in many aspects with their baths, forums, and brothels. Everyone could potentially participate on some level in the power and success enjoyed by the elite.

The elite constantly reminded the public of its power over the life and death of the inhabitants of the empire, allowing some level of participation in the popular public entertainment, which reinforced the assumptions of the system. "What was distinctive of Roman cities was the amphitheater. The amphitheater was like a death-camp extermination device located in the center of the city for the pleasure of the whole populace. People came out to enjoy the torment and death of living beings, human and non-human. Such physical violence distinctively replicated the chief product of the city; power sanctioned by force. People sat in hierarchical ranks to revel in the death of others."[12]

10. Ibid., 358.

11. Braudel, *Memory*, 48.

12. Malina, "Daily Life," 362. The capacity of the Roman public for bloody entertainment is the subject of much speculation by the "advanced" societies of the West. Is the spectacle of cruel death of humans and animals another example of the depravity of the Roman public at that time? Perhaps this is part of it. I prefer the analysis that has to do

Politics was about "the symboling of social relations in terms of vertical roles, statuses and interactions. Politics was about effective collective action, the application of force to attain collective goals. The roles, statuses, entitlements, and obligations of the political system were available to properly pedigreed persons from only the 'best' families, hence tied up with the kinship system."[13] The best of society institutionalized cruelty in order to keep dissenters in check and to intimidate those who attempted to resist. Note how good and evil are defined eventually by the "good" people. Evil, when utilized by the good people in the empire for good, *is* good.

Thus the public celebrations, the annual festivals on the birthday of the emperor, the religious rituals, and religiously oriented games of the empire were occasions when the population could participate in the stories and myths of the empire, the pagan system of which they were a part. This participation gave even those of low status a sense of identity. They might be slaves, but they belonged to the most powerful and glorious nation in history. Their personal hopes and dreams were linked to the promises of the empire. They could share, albeit in a very limited way, in its power, domination, and control.

So while the stratification divided the power and concentrated the rewards toward the top of the pyramid, the tantalizing possibility of rewards oriented the majority of the population toward cooperation and compliance. For those who recognized the futility of acquiescence, the emptiness of the promises, and the oppression of the system, the threat of death usually prevented overt resistance. "Good" violence of the military, utilized at the discretion of the rulers, ensured the compliance of the disenfranchised, the acceptance of their low status, and their role as producers for the elite. Violence and the threat of death protected the system that favored the few at the expense of the many.

---

with the vicarious triumph over death, the sense of purpose and justice that these spectacles engendered in the observers. We will look more closely at the life/death themes of the Roman Empire dramatized in gladiator combat in later chapters dealing with Paul's message of the resurrection. The entertaining drama of life and death are, of course, still very much part of the world today. Is modern violent entertainment and the reasons why people everywhere in the world avidly watch it (aside from the fact that people do not actually die, but just appear to) any different at all from gladiatorial combat?

13. Ibid., 358.

Perspectives on the Sea

The success of the Roman Empire was inextricably linked to understanding, utilizing, and dominating the Mediterranean Sea. Historian Fernand Braudel describes the historical significance of the Mediterranean well:

> It is in fact the major feature of the [Mediterranean] sea's destiny that it should be locked inside the largest group of landmasses on the globe, the "gigantic linked continent" of Europe-Asia-Africa, a sort of planet in itself, where goods and people circulated from earliest times. Human beings found a theater for their historical drama in these three conjoined continents. This was where the crucial exchanges took place.
>
> And since this human history was in perpetual motion, flowing down to the shores of the Mediterranean where it regularly came to a halt, is it any wonder that the sea should so soon have become one of the living centres of the universe?[14]

For the Hebrews in the biblical literature, all of which was written by people of the land until Luke wrote his Gospel and the Book of Acts, the sea was a foreign world. While the Mediterranean was a "sea of promise" for the people of the sea, for the Jewish people of the land it was primarily a "sea of peril." Fluid, changeable, capricious, and chaotic, the Mediterranean was viewed as an unpredictable counterpart to the permanence of the land, which represented so clearly the steadfast attributes of their God.

In contrast, numerous pagan gods were intimately connected with this sea, emerging out of it, expressing themselves in their anger or blessing in the sea, riding its waves, changing, hiding in its waters, and revealing themselves to humans who ventured into its waters in the forms of a variety of sea creatures. Could this be the reason that John the Revelator, writing from Patmos Island, surrounded by the sea, exults that "there was no more sea" in his vision of God's glorious defeat of rebellious empires (Rev 21:1)?

The characteristics of the pagan gods mirrored those of the sea. Both the sea and the gods are capricious, temperamental, beautiful, violent, sullen, and volatile. The images and reputation of the gods even traveled the sea on the trading and military vessels, competing with and eventually

14. Braudel, *Memory*, 15–16.

joining the existing local gods in a growing pantheon of Mediterranean deities. These sea-going gods shared common identities under a variety of local names. The sea carried the common promises of the various pagan gods offering personal power and success in all its forms; knowledge, beauty, victory, safety, health, wealth, pleasure, long life, honor, and status. For the people of the land, the seductive gods of the sea, like the sea itself, were perilous.

In contrast, the God of the Old Testament is faithful and changeless. God is a rock. This is a God who is neither described with sea metaphors nor is identified with the sea. God does not dwell in the seas as Poseidon, nor emerge from the sea as Aphrodite. In his third act of creation, God divides the water from the land. God calls this division good.

It is through the sea on *dry* land that God leads his people. Then fittingly, the sea destroys the Egyptian army. God meets Moses at the top of a mountain, and Moses receives God's commandments carved in stone. It is into and through the desert where God leads his people to the land where everlasting covenants will be realized. While this God may have power over all of nature, God almost always chooses to demonstrate his power on the land where his people belong.

The Land of Promise was and remains a land bridge between empires and continents. While living on the land bridge made life difficult for the small empire between the superpower of Egypt to the south and the various superpowers of the north, they were rooted in that land. Other invaders and enemies with their evil gods and ways came from the sea. Although some of God's people of the land occasionally "go down to the sea in ships" (Ps 107:23), it is usually their seaborne enemies who are mentioned in the Old Testament. Jonah flees to the sea to escape God. (Why does Jonah assume God is not there?) He suffers calamity at sea. (What else can you expect there?) Jonah learns his lesson.

Ezekiel 27, the classic ancient description of the sea, its potential and its peril, details the power and the glory of Tyre, which was contingent upon trade and the control of the shipping and harbors.[15] The people of

15. The discovery of two Iron Age shipwrecks off the coast of Israel in 1999 lends credence to the accurate description of Mediterranean shipping in Ezekiel 27. See Ballard and Stager, "Iron Age Shipwrecks," for a detailed report of this discovery and the clear evidence of the extent and importance of sea trade long before the Roman Empire secured the shipping and travel on the sea for its own interests.

the Mediterranean traded goods and gods, idols and ideas, and it is no accident that all of the cultures around the Mediterranean were polytheistic, for they shared their gods like they shared their products, adapting, borrowing, expanding the pantheon until it evolved and eventually supported the domination of the Roman Empire.

The people of the sea in the biblical story, like the sea itself, are full of promise and peril. The people of the land are tempted by the sea people's women and gods and are threatened by their military skill and technological superiority. For the land people of Israel, it was the sea from which the Phoenicians and the Philistines invaded with their sea-like gods. It was these sea people who controlled the harbors and the entire coastline of the land, keeping the Israelites in the hill country for most of biblical history. These technologically advanced people never were actually completely and finally defeated. The land may have been promised to the people of God, but the people of the sea with their gods successfully challenged the promise along the Mediterranean coast of the land.

Thus the fluid and chaotic Mediterranean was more than merely the means of transportation for the sea-based empires. It was the visible center, the cultural heart, the religious worldview of almost all of the empires that emerged around its rim. Although neutral in terms of what could be transported, the islands in the Mediterranean and the cities around its perimeter were linked together. This liquid connection enabled the islands and cities of the sea to become rich and powerful, as well as vulnerable to their sea-going enemies, as Ezekiel 27, mentioned above, graphically portrays. Braudel's description of the islands could be applied to the great cities of the Mediterranean as well: "They are extreme micro-universes, wide open to the outside world, vulnerable to invasions of people, technology and even fashion."[16]

Sea travel had become so safe and accessible by the first century that people could, for personal reasons such as health treatments and religious pilgrimages, or even out of ordinary curiosity, visit the famous sites, the power and triumph of kings and gods.[17] The sea was key to movement in the empire.

16. Braudel, *Memory,* 127.

17. One of the best studies on ancient travel is Lionel Casson's *Travel in the Ancient World.* Tony Perrottet's travelogue, *Pagan Holiday,* provides an entertaining insight into

Of the so-called Seven Wonders of Ancient World, the most famous list being compiled by the historian Heroditus, all except one, the Hanging Gardens of Babylon, were located around the rim of the Mediterranean. All were demonstrations of the power and triumph of gods, emperors, or both. Even the famous lighthouse of Alexandria at the harbor of Alexandria in Egypt, the only wonder that served a practical function, bore the inscription: "Dedicated to the Savior gods, on behalf of those who sail the seas." The Colossus of Rhodes, which may have straddled the entrance of the Mandraki Harbor on the Island of Rhodes, was dedicated to the sun god. Artemis's Temple at Ephesus, another harbor city, was the center of worship to the Ephesian Artemis. The Statue of Zeus at Olympia was dedicated to Zeus, the most powerful of the Greek gods. The Mausoleum at Halicarnassus (the modern port city of Bodrum, Turkey) was the final resting place for a king.

The most ancient, and the only one of the famous seven still visible, is the Great Pyramid of Giza, mentioned earlier. This tomb of pharaoh, as did all of the numerous pyramids built in Egypt over the years, had to do with the power of the gods to grant eternal life to the pharaoh. The pyramids were monuments that brought both the power and triumph of the empire and power and triumph of the gods together visibly.

While the sea provided the travel possibilities for the wealthy and curious of the Roman Empire to marvel at those Seven Wonders that were visible at the time, every major harbor around the Mediterranean was also a showcase of the power and success of the pagan empire of Rome. Temples to the gods and emperors, even in Caesarea in Palestine, dominated the high ground above many harbors, while others boasted spectacular temples literally at the waters' edge. Monuments commemorating the achievements of the emperors, as well as shopping areas and theaters immediately adjacent to the harbors, were common. The triumph of Rome, from the point of view of the sea traveler by the middle of the first century, must have seemed complete. The empire's expansion to the rest of the world must have seemed inevitable,[18] even to many Jews living in the stubborn Roman province of Palestine.

---

the tourist industry that was flourishing in the Mediterranean during the time of Paul.

18. Malina, "Daily Life," 370. Like others, Malina cites evidence that Rome did not have a grand plan of global conquest, but that there were widespread assumptions that

The Jewish Islands in the Mediterranean Empire

In the first century, Jews were living throughout the Roman Empire. Saul was one of these Diaspora Jews who would have made an occasional pilgrimage to Jerusalem in order to worship in the temple there. Saul and any other Jew on pilgrimage to Jerusalem could not have failed to notice, as they arrived by ship into one of the ports of Palestine, the splendid temples of the gods. These temples were built for the gods who enabled the Roman occupiers to triumph over the Jews, the people dedicated to the God they were coming to worship in Jerusalem.

The Jews were the stubborn, proud, humiliated stumbling block to the power and the triumph of the Roman Empire. The monotheistic Jewish communities formed religious and cultural islands in the pagan sea. While tolerated and included within the amazing variety of ethnic groups, languages, and religions that made up the Roman Empire in the first century, there was a latent and sometimes overt threat toward the non-conforming contradiction of Judaism. Judaism threatened the unity of the faith system of the empire. This threat was not limited to Palestine. With the relative safety and ease of travel on both land and sea, Jewish communities could be found throughout the empire. In spite of the fact that Jews too could be citizens, and could even choose to become completely Hellenized, these communities of contradiction continued to generate both hostility and admiration throughout the empire. The Jews posed a threat to Rome, for these exclusive land people and their exclusive land God would never be completely reliable and compliant citizens of the Rome.

Jesus, the Jew, was born, lived, taught, and was crucified within this reality. His ministry, centered primarily on and around the miniature Mediterranean, the Sea of Galilee, demonstrated the potential universal appeal of Jesus' message within the empire around the Mediterranean. The realization of this potential however, brings us again to the Book of Acts, in Jerusalem, the center of the monotheistic faith of the Judaism. "You will be my witnesses," Jesus promised his disciples at his farewell, "in Jerusalem, in all Judea and Samaria, and to the ends of the earth" (Acts

---

the power and goodness of Rome made universal triumph inevitable. We will look at the parallel assumptions with contemporary globalization in a later chapter.

1:8). The disciples knew that they were in Jerusalem at the moment,[19] and that they had been with Jesus in Judea and Samaria. But what must have unsettled them the most was the prospect of representing Jesus and the kingdom of God to the "ends of the earth." The ends of the earth were where pagans lived. The ends of the earth began right at the seaports like Caesarea along the shore of the Mediterranean. The port city of Caesarea was one place they had never been with Jesus, but they would likely have heard reports of the overwhelming power and scandalous pagan presence of Rome on display there.

They were aware that the kingdom, or *basilea*, of God, to which they had been attracted by Jesus, seemed to be very different than the powerful, pagan *basilea* of Rome under which they lived, or the temple-centered *basilea* remembered or anticipated by the Jews of Palestine. The three years they had been following Jesus had been marked by those very things most people seek to avoid and empire builders promise to reduce or eliminate—insecurity, unpredictability, instability, humiliation, and even defeat. They had constantly been on the move with Jesus during the previous three years following him throughout the Galilee, Samaria, and Judea. They had experienced the volatile combination of adulation and hostility from the crowds in villages and especially in Jerusalem. They had sailed the Sea of Galilee with Jesus through life-threatening gales visiting foreign territories where they might meet, on the same afternoon, people or pigs possessed by demons.

Before we examine how Paul continued and expanded this extraordinary movement toward the kingdom of God in the empire on and around the Mediterranean Sea, we'll look at Jesus' power, promises, and demonstration of this unstable and insecure movement on and around the Sea of Galilee.

---

19. While this text is often used to demonstrate that sharing the good news should begin at home, Jerusalem was not home to the disciples. It was an unfamiliar and even dangerous place for them. In fact, none of the places Jesus mentioned was home. All the places were to some extent unfamiliar and intimidating places in which to witness, the "ends of the earth" especially so.

part 2

The Church Is Like a Ship at Sea

SAILINGACTS, LIKE ALL GOOD old sailboats, is designed to provide a relatively safe and comfortable home, even on dangerous and rolling seas. Although at times, when heeled over in a gale with water and spray flying everywhere, the sailboat does not feel all that safe and is certainly not comfortable. But after proving time and again to be rugged and dependable in all kinds of weather, we have learned to trust the boat. The boat is our home.

I discovered, as I attempted to back into a Mediterranean-style berth for the first time, that *SailingActs*, like most sailboats, is not designed to go backward. Under sail it can only move ahead. Using the power of the motor forces the boat to move backward, but like a stubborn two-year-old it behaves erratically, kicking sideways, totally uncooperative.

I also learned it is only when there is balanced tension between the weight of the keel and the wind in the sails that the sailboat makes good progress. It is the balance between the weight below the water and the wind above the surface that creates the beautiful, exhilarating forward rush across the water. If sailboats had no keel or other means of counterbalance, they would capsize. If they had no sail, they would never move or would simply drift along in whatever direction the wind was blowing. Both keel and sail are absolutely necessary for voyaging. If the keel or the sail were human, neither could say to the other, "I have no need of you" just because of the tension between the two. Balanced tension results in positive progress towards the destination.

Paul spent many days, weeks, and months aboard small coastal cargo ships plying the Mediterranean on his travels. Paul was a man of the sea, and I believe that as Paul sailed on these ships he recognized the way that the new Christian communities emerging in the port cities of the Mediterranean resembled ships at sea. But the ship-like features of the Christian movement in the Mediterranean had started with Jesus and his followers on and around the Sea of Galilee.

3

The Jesus Movement
and the Sea of Galilee

The Kingdom That Contradicts

IN THE FIRST CENTURY it was the Roman Empire that had occupied and subjugated the peoples around the Mediterranean Sea, including the supposedly God-protected people of Israel. The power of Rome was felt and the triumph of Rome was seen everywhere around the rim of the entire Mediterranean Sea. Liberation from the rule of Rome and restoration of the kingdom in some form or another was at the top of the national popular agenda within Palestine. Zealots, Pharisees, Herodians, and Sadducees all dreamed of a powerful and glorious Israel, all developed their systems of dichotomization, all made their promises and threats based on their particular knowledge of good and evil. The common people listened and dreamed of a better day. It was into this world of dazzling, conflicting visions and dismal realities that Jesus of Nazareth came "proclaiming the good news of the kingdom" (Matt 4:23b).

I often take my cross-cultural students from Eastern Mennonite University part way up the hill of the traditional site of the Sermon on the Mount, on the north end of the Sea of Galilee, to read and listen to Jesus' words in context.

Let us imagine for a moment that we are on that hill at the north end of the Sea of Galilee, listening to Jesus teach. It is a clear day. We can see the entire shoreline of the small lake in the panorama below. What could Jesus and his listeners have seen as they looked south that day? The sparkling water of the Galilee is dotted with the crude fishing boats used by the Jewish fishermen from Capernaum and other fishing villages. The listeners from Capernaum could easily pick out their own houses. The Roman military camp next to their town could be clearly seen close to the water's edge.

Looking left, they could look over into the territory ruled by Philip, the son of Herod the Great, spreading out at the foot of Mount Hermon and up the slopes of the Golan. To the southeast, down the shore of the lake, they could see where the area of Decapolis began with its magnificent Hellenistic cities. To the right, looking southwest, the new Roman city of Tiberias, with its bath and walls, dedicated to the Roman Caesar and still under construction, could be seen. The rugged cliffs of Arbel, jutting majestically up from the lake shore just a little farther right, was a reminder of the defeat of the Zealot holdouts in their caves at the end of the Jewish War against the Roman forces under Herod the Great just some sixty years or so earlier. Every direction Jesus' listeners looked reinforced their awareness that Rome was in control, not them. They were just poor peasants with little to lose by following Jesus.

Blessed are the poor, the sorrowful, the meek, the hungry and thirsty, the merciful, the pure in heart, the peacemakers, and the persecuted, Jesus told the fishermen and other peasants on the hill overlooking the wealth, triumph, pride, injustice, and selfishness of the corrupt and violent oppressors building Roman Tiberias. You will inherit the earth. The kingdom belongs to you (Matt 5:3–10). "Your kingdom come," Jesus taught his disciples to pray, "your will be done on earth as it is in heaven" (6:9b–10). While Tiberias was visible to Jesus' listeners that day on the mountain, Jerusalem, the city built around the temple, the political capital and spiritual center of David's kingdom, was not. Jesus' definition of the kingdom however, contradicted the quest for and achievement of power and control displayed in both of these cities.

The Movement on Land and Sea

Nazareth, Jesus' home village of perhaps four hundred inhabitants in the first century, is situated almost exactly halfway between the Mediterranean Sea to the west and the Sea of Galilee to the east. It was a typical, very rural peasant village. But although Nazareth was landlocked, the young Jesus certainly had seen the Mediterranean, perhaps in his early travels to Egypt, but much more likely as a boy in Nazareth. A short, steep hike to the top of the Nazareth Ridge provides a view of the Mediterranean. From there, on a clear day, Jesus could have even seen the sails of the boats making their way up and down the coast between the ports of Caesarea to the south and Tyre to the north.

Today in Nazareth Village, a project of the local Christian community of Nazareth, one can visit a replica of the Nazareth in which Jesus spent the majority of his life. This carefully researched village in the heart of modern Nazareth allows the visitor to examine the living conditions typical of a small, poor Jewish village in the Galilee. With its simple stone houses with dirt floors and outdoor courtyards for cooking, living, and working, the terraced fields, the sheep, goats, and donkeys wandering by, the olive press, and the synagogue, Nazareth Village depicts the humble village life that shaped Jesus' boyhood knowledge of the world.

Another extremely valuable resource for insight into the world of Jesus' youth and his ministry as an adult is the Jesus Trail. This recently completed four-day walking trail, which begins in Nazareth and ends in Capernaum, allows the visitor to experience the effort of moving through the Galilee by foot. The Jesus Trail, leading through Arab villages and Jewish farming communities, through Muslim, Christian, and Jewish neighborhoods, through poverty and affluence, through power and weakness, allows the hiker today to experience the diversity of Galilee in the time of Jesus and the social tensions through which Jesus regularly walked on his journeys across the Galilee.

The university study program I lead always includes time in both Nazareth Village and four days hiking the entire length of the Jesus Trail. Inevitably questions emerge: "Why did Jesus, raised in rural Nazareth, choose the Sea of Galilee for the center of his ministry?" The Sea of Galilee plays virtually no role in Scripture until Jesus. It is briefly mentioned in the Old Testament but only as a natural boundary of the inheritance for one of the tribes. For the people of the land, the Sea of Galilee is largely irrelevant. Yet Jesus focused on the people living around the Sea of Galilee for his ministry.

Why did Jesus choose Capernaum, a small fishing harbor, as his base or "home port"? Tiberias, the Roman city being built on the water's edge, with its baths, theater, and pagan temples, visible to anyone using a boat anywhere on the Sea of Galilee, is not even mentioned once by Jesus. For Jesus, Tiberias is irrelevant. But why chose Capernaum?

Why did Jesus call fishermen as his followers? Jewish fishermen are rare in Jewish literature and not mentioned at all in the Old Testament. In the first century, fishermen were considered as having very low status, partly because they were almost always ritually unclean due to the unclean fish they regularly had to handle, and because of the unclean people around the Sea of Galilee with whom they did business. Tax collectors and other authorities mistrusted fishermen, for with boats it was possible to avoid taxes when crossing the territorial borders around the Sea of Galilee.

And why did several of these very same minimally educated, unclean, and unruly fishermen whom Jesus called as disciples become the key leaders of the movement following Jesus' crucifixion, resurrection, and ascension?

Let us consider some possibilities. The Sea of Galilee at the time of Jesus could be described as a miniature version of the Mediterranean Sea. In a matter of hours one could sail from Judaism to paganism, from poverty to wealth, from oppression to domination, from weakness to power, from humility to glory and back again. A careful look at a good Bible atlas reveals that at the time of Jesus the Sea of Galilee connected three main political territories. On the west and north was Galilee, a region of mixed population including a diversity of Jews, Romans, and Samaritans. To the north and east was the territory governed by Herod the Great's son Philip, with its city of Caesarea Philippi, which contained a pagan temple dedicated to the god Pan, as well as other temples. To the east and south was the region of Decapolis, with its Hellenistic and Roman cities and non-Jewish populations, some of whom raised pigs.

Could it be that Jesus, following the temptations in the desert, began in the Capernaum area with initial success, then upon encountering the violent, almost lethal resistance to his Nazareth synagogue message, recognized the relative openness to the people around the Sea of Galilee compared to landlocked Nazareth? The Nazareth synagogue message, after all, had touched off resistance not because of the promises Jesus made about himself fulfilling the vision of Isaiah immediately (Luke 4:22), but because Jesus inferred that non-Jews were to be included in the promises. At the very beginning of Jesus' ministry, it seems that the closer he got to the water that connected people to the world's diversity, the more receptive people were. Of the population centers in Palestine, Jerusalem, located high above sea level, is the major city most isolated from the seaports. Jerusalem is also the most conservative, controlling, resistant, and dangerous place Jesus ministers. Paul later discovers the same about Jerusalem in his ministry.

Could it be that Jesus recognized that people growing up close to the water might be the most open to learn about the kingdom? Did Jesus consider the relational skills of the people around the Sea of Galilee, who were used to interacting with non-Jews, as being potentially effective skills for representing and leading the movement of the kingdom in the Galilee and eventually throughout the Roman Empire?

Jesus Defines the Kingdom in the Empire

The Sea of Galilee then, is where the contrasting promises of Jesus and the kingdom of God and those of Tiberias and the Roman Empire interact. As a reminder, the New Testament Greek word *basilea*, used consistently in Jesus' teachings about the kingdom of God, is the only word used for "kingdom" in the New Testament, either for the kingdoms of the world, such as the Roman Empire, or the kingdom of God. Carter points out that one could just as well speak of the "kingdom of Rome" or the "empire of God." Linguistically, there is no differentiation between political and spiritual kingdoms in the New Testament.[1]

Carter, like other recent scholars, draws attention to a number of Jesus' actions and words that seem to directly challenge both Herod's claims as "king of the Jews" and the Caesars' claims of "Lord." Whether or not Jesus deliberately focused his message and actions to include politi-

1. Carter, *Matthew and Empire*, 5.

cal and prophetic challenge to the Roman Empire is a matter of debate. But there is no question that Jesus' teaching about the kingdom of God and his actions, which demonstrated the way it would come into being, contradicted the power and obvious achievements of the Roman Empire and addressed the permanent, universal temptation of empire building for personal and collective power and control.

Jesus' life had begun under the rule of Herod the Great and was impacted from birth by Herod's paranoid power. Jesus' early childhood in Egypt may well have left him with memories of the pyramids, the temples, and other monuments of the former power and domination of the Egyptian Empire. Contrary to popular imagination, Jesus' boyhood in Nazareth was not one of naïve, rural isolation. The boy Jesus observed more than just the sailboats on the Mediterranean from the Nazareth Ridge, for the region of Galilee was permeated by Hellenistic and Roman influence. Showcases of the power and success of the pagan culture were as close as Sepphoris, the beautiful, wealthy, Hellenized town only four miles away from Nazareth.[2] Travelers and caravaners passed close by Nazareth as they followed one of the main trade routes through the Jezreel Valley from the sea coast, or on the north side of the Nazareth Ridge, carrying with them not only the goods from afar, but also the tales of the wonders of other empires to the east. During Jesus' lifetime, Herod Antipas had built well-known luxury palaces in the Galilee, Sepphoris, and Tiberias. The kingdoms of the world had always paraded through the Galilee on their way to make war or to trade with others. And Rome, the greatest warring and trading empire, was on permanent display during Jesus' entire life.

It is in the context of the success of the Roman occupiers on display in Palestine that Jesus' temptation in the wilderness is best understood. While the location of the temptations is preserved in church tradition only, one can assume from the description in the Gospels and the landscape of Palestine that Jesus was likely in or beyond the Jordan valley

---

2. There is credible evidence that Jesus was familiar with Sepphoris, its wealth, its pagan lifestyle, theaters, and villas, its power and glory. The argument that Joseph may have found work in Sepphoris, with Jesus as his helper, is made by a number of authors, but none more fascinating than by Richard Batey in his book *Jesus & the Forgotten City*. See pp. 65–82 for his presentation of the evidence.

toward the Dead Sea, a region so desolate, dry, and inhospitable that one could preserve a parchment scroll in a cave there for two thousand years.

As mentioned earlier, Herod the Great, the self-designated "king of the Jews," loved to place his palaces and fortresses in areas like those of the temptation of Jesus. Jesus not only saw at least some of these symbols of power and domination, he may have been within viewing distance of one or more of these palatial displays of Herod's self-importance during his actual temptation.

Jesus, then, was familiar with the kingdoms of the world with which Satan tempted him. All of the temptations were for power, control, and triumph. All of the temptations were about utilizing the power of good for good. All came with attractive, credible promises. The temptations promised that Jesus, like the first humans, could also be as God, utilizing good and evil to establish the kingdom of God. Jesus was being tempted to rise to the top of the pyramid, his rightful place, and from there to rule the kingdom of God as everyone expected the Messiah to do.[3]

Unlike the first humans, Jesus rejected this permanent and universal temptation to establish a kingdom, even the kingdom of God, according to the patterns of human empire building. The fact that he could have done this through the exercise of his power, and could have triumphed and received glory rather than experiencing defeat, inevitable humiliation, and death because of the prophetic and revolutionary path he chose, makes Jesus' resistance an incredible feat of victory.

Jesus' announcement and demonstration of the kingdom of God contrasts with the patterns of both the Roman Empire and the hierarchical power structures of the Jewish religious establishment. Jesus orients his followers not toward the familiar and rigid top of the social pyramid, but toward the uncertain and unstable future. The promises of the kingdom defy the present patterns of human exploitive relationships and oppressive organization, and can be depicted as follows.

3. For a discussion of the political implications inherent in the temptation of Jesus in the wilderness, see Yoder's *Politics*, 24–27.

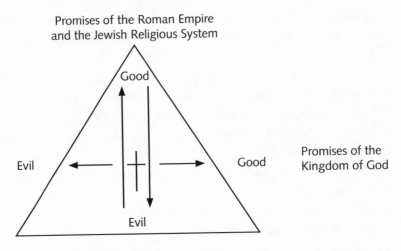

FIGURE 3.1. Jesus Representing the Kingdom within the Roman Empire

From the diagram, several observations can be made about the relationship of Jesus and the kingdom of God to human hierarchical patterns of good and evil and systems of control and domination. Jesus' teaching, his life, and his death all demonstrate a consistent alternative approach to establishing the kingdom of God. Jesus' approach reflects the tradition of the Hebrew prophets who "troubled" the kings of Israel and begged the people not to put their trust in the rulers of their powerful neighbors.

The social position from which Jesus ministered, taught, and led his followers was not at the top, exercising power derived from status within the good, but rather closer to the bottom, close to the poor, those who hungered and thirsted for justice, the oppressed and exploited. It was the social position of Moses, who, although a prince of Egypt, identified with the slaves, challenging the pharaoh and leading the people toward the promised freedom. Were Moses and the prophets "good" according to the political and religious systems of measurement? Your ancestors "murdered the prophets," Jesus reminded the religious authorities of his day (Matt 23:31).

Not only did Jesus reject the power that he could have attained by achieving and utilizing good within the system of good and evil, he indicated that the system itself was flawed and irrelevant. "Why do you call me good?" Jesus asked the rich young ruler. "No one is good but God alone"

(Luke 18:19). Was Jesus not good? That is not the point he was making. He was debunking the elaborate, inconsistent system of measuring good developed by those in authority and used by them to control others for their own benefit. God alone, not humans with their self-interested knowledge of good and evil, identifies the good. Good, in Jesus' demonstration and teaching, is defined as orientation towards the kingdom of God. Evil is turning back, going away from the kingdom of God.

The content of Jesus' teaching and the pattern of his actions were consistently prophetic and relevant to both the system of Jewish religious life and the Roman occupation, and provided an alternative to the promises of both. Looking first at the Jewish system of religious dichotomization, Jesus uses the familiar categories "righteous/sinner," "rich/poor," 'wise/foolish," "clean/unclean," and "healthy/sick" when describing good and evil. However, instead of reinforcing the patterns of division according to the official consensus, in norm-shattering fashion he inverts and redefines the categories. "Blessed are you who are poor . . . but woe to you who are rich" (Luke 6:20, 24). The good Pharisees look clean on the outside, but inwardly they are "full of the bones of the dead and all kinds of filth" (Matt 23:27).

By inverting and redefining the good/evil categories, Jesus threatened the status quo at every level and raised the hopes of those relegated by life's circumstances or their own actions toward the bottom of the social hierarchy. Jesus' message was an invitation for these people to follow him in a radically new direction toward the promise of abundant and eternal life, the promise of the kingdom of God. "I am the way, and the truth, and the life," he proclaimed (John 14:6). Implicit in his actions, and occasionally explicit in his teachings, was the promise of liberation from the tyranny of the quest for knowledge, power, and domination, the necessity and compulsion to judge, and most importantly, the power and fear of death itself. Jesus promised life in abundance, life eternal.

What a list of liberations! What a list of promises! Why would anyone in first-century Palestine not choose to follow Jesus? It is not hard to imagine why the peasants were attracted to these promises. It is also easy to understand why those on the top of the social pyramid were just as likely to reject Jesus' description and demonstration of the kingdom of God. They had, as Jesus commented, already received the rewards of those who were deemed good within the system: status, honor, wealth, power, influence, respect, comfort, and satisfaction. But for the majority of people in first-century Palestine on the lower levels of the social pyramid, the promises of Jesus for life in abundance in the present followed by eternal life in the future, the attraction was far greater.

There were, of course, risks as well for the people toward the bottom of the pyramid who believed Jesus' promises and began to follow him toward the coming kingdom. The risk of losing what little they had, the risk of suffering even more, the risk of being ostracized and condemned by the religious authorities, and the risk of attracting the suspicious attention of the Roman authorities were all very real. Living by a vision that contradicts the organized power of human kingdoms is always risky and sometimes lethal. The biblical understanding of this vision-oriented life, Brueggemann has noted, is "the double process of turning loose from the way things are and embracing in *great risk* the way God has promised they will be."[4]

The promises of the religious and political leaders, who displayed impressive power and success in first-century Palestine of the Roman Empire, competed with the promises of Jesus. The promises of both were attractive. Both could be demonstrated. But unlike the power exercised by the religious and especially the political rulers, Jesus did not exercise coercive and threatening power. How could he establish a kingdom with voluntary followers who, when they associated with Jesus, risked attracting the negative attention of both political and religious leaders? Unlike Jesus, those leaders possessed and exercised the power to punish and reward and were ready to use it when necessary.

Listen to Jesus' realistic promise to his followers just after the rich young ruler, upon learning that he would need to liquidate his assets and give the proceeds to the poor, had decided not to follow Jesus. Peter, apparently feeling very righteous at the moment for leaving his meager fishing equipment behind, had said to Jesus, "We have left everything to follow you!"

"Truly I tell you," Jesus replied, "there is no one who has left house or brothers or sisters or mother or father or children or fields, for my sake and for the sake of the good news, who will not receive a hundredfold now

---

4. Brueggemann, *Bible Makes Sense,* 93 (emphasis added).

in this age—houses, brothers and sisters, mothers and children, and fields with persecutions—and in the age to come eternal life" (Mark 10:28–30).

The rich young ruler, a good man toward the top of the pyramid, was socially far above Peter, but Jesus did not conclude his comments as one might expect. Instead of telling Peter, "those on the bottom will be on top, and the top on the bottom," which would have been startling enough, he said instead, "But many who are first will be last, and the last first." The kingdom of God is not vertically oriented with power and authority exercised hierarchically. The kingdom of God is horizontally oriented. You can be first and last in the kingdom of God, but ranking above and below in the kingdom of God is inherently contradictory to the good news of the kingdom.

This is clear in what immediately happened. Following the story of the rich young ruler, when James and John asked for high status positions in the future kingdom of Jesus, Jesus replied, "You know that among Gentiles those whom they recognize as their rulers lord it over them, and their great ones are tyrants over them. But it is not so among you; but whoever wishes to become great among you must be your servant" (Mark 10:42–43).

The Social Dynamics of the Movement of the Kingdom of God

The social movement of the kingdom of God was therefore not an "upside down kingdom"[5] that inverts the order of the kingdoms of the world, but one that both intersects with and challenges the good/evil patterns of society and offers a fundamentally different way of living, of organizing life, and relating socially. Power is still operative in the kingdom of God, but it is not exercised in expected ways that reinforce the fundamentally divisive, inequitable, and oppressive patterns of society. The following diagram depicts the dynamic shape of the Jesus' movement of life toward the promises of the kingdom.

---

5. This observation in no way is meant to criticize the concept of "the upside down kingdom" popularized by Donald Kraybill's excellent book with that title. The contrasts between Jesus' teaching and the social and religious expectation of the authorities are sharp enough to be called "upside down." Indeed, Paul was accused of "turning the world upside down" with his preaching.

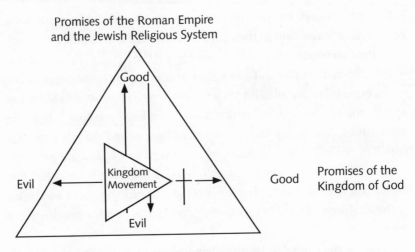

FIGURE 3.2. The Movement of the Kingdom in Palestine: Orientation and Shape

The distinctive feature of *movement* of Jesus and his followers toward the kingdom of God cannot be overstated. While the movement of the kingdom is future-oriented, the effects are immediate. Shaped by hope and faith in Jesus' promises, those who follow Jesus are conspicuously visible, attractive, threatening, and always relevant. The shape of the kingdom of God fits neither the shape of the Roman Empire nor the shape of the social/political/religious Jewish system within it. The followers of Jesus on their way to the promise of the kingdom form, in the New Testament description, a community of life in abundance, which includes suffering now and the promise of eternal life in the future.

This is a movement of the kingdom toward the promises of the coming kingdom. It embodies the hope and life of the future kingdom. It is in the world, but it is unlike the kingdoms of the world for this movement does not reflect the familiar patterns of power and domination that shape human relationships and organization. It is the movement of abundant life toward eternal life.

The diagram above depicts the choice of two ways described by Jesus. "The gate is wide and the road is easy that leads to destruction, and there are many who take it," Jesus taught. But "the gate is narrow and the road is hard that leads to life, and there are few who find it" (Matt 7:13–14). The horizontal line represents movement following Jesus, the way, the truth, and the life, on the road that leads to life described by Jesus.

The diagram also demonstrates the easy way that leads to death. While the easy road has two possibilities which seemingly lead in opposite directions, to the consternation of those who have defined, chosen, and achieved the good, neither direction on the easy way leads to life. The good and evil ways of humans are really two lanes ultimately leading to the same destination. Neither direction leads to life. Both end in death.

The suffering inherent in the cross-movement of Jesus, the movement that cuts across the cultural patterns that organize, divide, and control society, is also clear from the diagram. This cross-movement places the followers of Jesus, like Jesus himself, in a position of both potential popularity and high risk. Like trying to cross a busy interstate highway with traffic speeding in both directions, navigating Palestine and the Roman Empire across the heavy religious, political, military, and social traffic patterns of good and evil was hazardous. One could get run over from either direction, with similar results. Both the good and the evil travelers on the broad ways of cultural patterns dislike being delayed by the construction zones of the kingdom of God, or the "Slow, Jesus' Follower Crossing" signs. Not all are willing to slow down on their urgent appointments with death, or ready to dodge the pedestrian traffic on the narrow way toward the kingdom. Traffic jams on the broad way are messy, sometimes deadly affairs, and those on the narrow way who are causing them as they cross the broad way will need to be ready, not only for the possibility of getting run over, but of being prosecuted afterwards by the authorities for impeding social progress, especially towards the popular "good" goals of society.

Promises and Power: Jesus' and Rome's

If the direction and social patterns of the kingdom of God are unlike human organizations, what about power? The power demonstrated by Jesus is operative among the followers in the kingdom of God in the world. "All authority in heaven and on earth has been given to me," Jesus told his followers on the occasion of his imminent departure. "Go therefore [connoting the spatial and social movement through the world, toward the kingdom] and make disciples of all nations [cultures, ethnic groups, tribes, nations]" (Matt 28:18–19). "You will receive power" for this task, Jesus promised at his farewell (Acts 1:8). All of the regions Jesus mentioned where his empowered witnesses would go—Jerusalem, Judea, Samaria, and to the ends of the earth—were regions under the authority and power of the Roman Empire.[6]

The movement toward the kingdom requires the power of God that was operative in Jesus. The power Jesus demonstrated was power to forgive, to love, to heal, to bind and loose, to serve, to make peace, to live free from the constrictive and destructive patterns of social organization, and to confront evil and overcome evil with good. The power of the kingdom in the world is the power demonstrated by Jesus in his life in the Roman Empire.

Never does the power exercised by Jesus include the exercise of coercive power common to those at the top of the pyramid. Jesus' power is exercised in a way that confronts evil but does not coerce or intimidate humans with lethal violence or the threat of it, or oppression of any kind. Jesus leads his followers as a shepherd leads his flock of sheep. Any follower of Jesus exercising power in ways that contradict Jesus' example and teaching is sinning in the same way as Adam and Eve in the story of the fall. One cannot exercise human power that is overtly or latently violent in the name of Jesus. To do so is blasphemy.

The power of the cross and the resurrection underlies the exercise of power of Jesus' followers in the world. It is the power of life that liberates from the fear of death. It is the power that cannot be intimidated into silence or inaction in the face of good promises of reward or evil threats and sanctions. The fear of loss of status is diminished. Love can triumph over fear, and the power of love, demonstrated on the cross, is the most powerful of all within human relationships.

The power operative in the kingdom of God in the example of Jesus is the opposite of both weakness and violent resistance. It is the bold exercise of power in defeat, demonstrated by those who flaunt their loss of social status in a way that empowers the weak and defeated in human society. Power for Jesus' followers in a world shaped by coercive and seduc-

---

6. That is, the regions to the west. Several of Jesus' disciples went east as well, outside of the Roman Empire, but their mission stories are not included in Scripture. In any case, wherever the ends of the earth to which the apostles went, their witness of the kingdom of God was in the context of empire.

tive power of empire was contingent on their utter reliance on the living Jesus. This kind of power could be called prophetic power, the ability to explain the truth, to demonstrate the promises, and to embody the vision, because of faith in the resurrection.

Jesus embodied the good news. He made the kingdom of God powerfully relevant, immediate, attractive, and accessible. When the people looked at Jesus, they saw the reality of the promises. When they looked at Jesus, they saw the kingdom of God. It was the clarity of the promises that attracted some and alarmed others. The promises of risk, suffering, humility, precariousness, and instability of the kingdom of God defined in Jesus' teaching and example stood in sharp contrast to the power, triumph, control and stability promised and demonstrated by both the Roman Empire and the Jewish religious system of Jesus' day.

It is clear that the promises of the kingdom contradicted those of empire. But did these promises and demonstrations of power and domination *connect* with the power and domination of the Roman Empire? If so, how? How could Jesus' alternative vision of the kingdom of God, with the cross, with the power exercised in giving and serving, with the egalitarian relationships, with the redefined triumph of suffering, how could all of this compete with the promises of power, control, and abundance in life that the empire demonstrated and offered? How could Jesus' promises of this kind of kingdom attract people who lived far from the Galilee, people who were surrounded by the real and immediate power and domination of the pagan Roman Empire?

The task of spreading the good news of Jesus' vision of the kingdom of God in the Roman Empire, where Caesar's power and glory dominated, was up to Jesus' followers. Jesus had represented the kingdom of God in Palestine, a small province of Rome, primarily among Jews who were a monotheistic minority in a polytheistic, pagan world. It would be up to others to take this message throughout the empire. They would need to go to sea.

From the Land to the Sea

As Luke writes in Acts, the shift from the Sea of Galilee to the Mediterranean Sea is startlingly swift for the group of disciples, people of the land, but a group that significantly also included several people of the tiny Sea of Galilee. The decisive move from land to sea was launched at Pentecost. The feast of Pentecost was one of the three annual pilgrim feasts when Jewish males were required to worship at the temple in Jerusalem. For the Jews living throughout the empire scattered as they were around the Mediterranean, travel to Palestine presented severe challenges.

In the first century, as is the case even today in the Mediterranean, the sailing season begins in May and ends in late October. The months between are prone to violent winter storms. Passover, the first of the three pilgrim festivals, was celebrated in the spring, a little early for safe and reliable ship transportation to the Palestine for the Jewish communities in Diaspora. The other pilgrim festival, Succoth, or the Feast of Tabernacles, was celebrated in the fall, too late in the sailing season to risk sea travel. Pentecost, fifty days after Passover, was and still is generally perfect sailing weather, and indeed this pilgrim festival drew the highest numbers of Jews living around the Mediterranean to Jerusalem. At Pentecost, Jews from the "ends of the earth" were in Jerusalem, a veritable wave of humanity from the empire.[7] The sea enabled many of these Jews to live far from Jerusalem and still fulfill at least part of their pilgrimage obligations.

Peter's address to the gathered Jews of the Diaspora, who were more than a little familiar with the power and triumph of Rome, included references to Jesus' power and triumph in the resurrection. This must have sounded especially shocking to the residents of the empire in Jerusalem for Pentecost, especially when Peter connected Jesus' kingdom to David's kingdom in his explanatory, prophetic sermon. The listeners would not soon forget this sermon, and would return to their homes in the Diaspora and share their experiences and questions within the Jewish communities of the empire.

In the next several chapters of Acts there follows a sweeping story of movement, confrontations, explanations, and people with non-Jewish names playing key roles. It is the people mentioned in the early chapters of Acts and the places from which they came which are intriguing. "There was a Levite, a native of Cyprus." Cyprus was an incredibly powerful,

---

7. A number of the regions listed in Acts 2:9–11 are linked to Jerusalem by the Mediterranean Sea. The people from these areas most likely traveled to Israel by sea ships owned and operated by pagans. They had no other choice.

wealthy, and thoroughly pagan island and a famous center of Aphrodite worship. The apostles called him Barnabas (Acts 4:36).

The seven deacons chosen to help with the distribution of food among the Hellenized Jewish widows in Jerusalem are themselves, as their names indicate, Hellenized Jews. One is even a Gentile convert to Judaism who comes from Antioch, a model city of Rome's power and success rivaling Rome and Alexandria (6:1–6). Another of the newly selected deacons, Stephen, quickly engages other Hellenized Jews in debate, and ends up at a hearing before the Sanhedrin for his efforts. His speech, in which he makes the case for the relative unimportance of the land and the temple in Jerusalem, earns him the death penalty (6:8—7:60).

The shift is relentlessly toward the Mediterranean Sea. Philip, another of the selected deacons preaches in Samaria, then is directed to go down toward Gaza, the old Philistine city on the shore of the Mediterranean (8:26). After his encounter with the Ethiopian courtier on his way back home, Philip ends up in Caesarea, the pagan Roman port city, the gateway to Rome in the land, built by Herod the Great. A pagan temple dominated the harbor. Philip is already at the ends of the earth (8:27).

The story of Peter and Cornelius in Acts 10 completes the move toward the sea, not just geographically, but socially and theologically as well. The story begins with Cornelius, a gentile attracted to Judaism and a centurion of the "Italian Regiment." He is stationed in Caesarea and lives among representatives of Roman rule and various other sea invaders. Peter is in Joppa, another of the very few seaports of the land. As Cornelius is being directed to send for Peter in Joppa, Peter is receiving a vision that will prepare him for one of the most important meetings in the history of the Jesus movement. Peter, on the roof of the house, sees "something like a large sheet" (10:11) coming down from, of all places, *heaven*, full of non-kosher animals.

The details are significant here. Remember, the invasion of unclean food and practices of the Gentiles is seen to come from the sea, not from heaven. And this sheet, which for modern readers might conjure up images of a bed sheet—something not used in first-century Palestine—can be interpreted as a "billowing sail," for the Greek word used in the story, *othonay*, refers either to a linen cloth or to a sail. To think of the sheet as a sail is consistent with the content of the story and descriptive of the square linen sails used in the first century. The vision then, not only gets Peter to accept Cornelius. Because the vision represents so clearly the sea invasion of the strange Greeks and Romans with their pagan practices and unclean cuisine, it helps the early Christian community, which now includes Hellenistic Jews from around the empire, to accept the peoples and cultures of the Mediterranean Sea. This is an incredibly important shift that sets the stage for the primary actor in Acts, Paul, the apostle to the Gentiles.

We return to Stephen's execution, where we first read of the young man Saul who is guarding the outer clothes of those who are doing the actual stoning of Stephen (7:54—8:1). While very brief in detail, several key insights into Saul's later conversion and ministry are offered here. Earlier, members of the Sanhedrin stared intently at Stephen as he testified, for "they saw that his face was like the face of an angel" (6:15). Is it not possible that, unlike the others who covered their ears, shouted, and rushed to kill Stephen when he described his glimpse into heaven, Saul was one of those who were watching everything intently? Is it not likely that Saul had caught a glimpse of Stephen's glowing face and perhaps was reminded of the face of Moses after his close encounter with God on Mt. Sinai? Is it not probable that Saul was troubled and curious during the stoning and the following days as he continued to mull over the visible and audible witness of Stephen?

What did Stephen describe that Saul could not forget? "Look," Stephen had exclaimed, "I see the heavens open and the Son of Man standing at the right hand of God!" (7:56). It is likely that Saul could not forget Stephen's unsettling view of Jesus, for he must have related that story to Luke after his own encounter with the living Lord. The impact at that time had to do with two insights that Stephen had within minutes of his death. One insight is the reality of God's power and glory, which would not have surprised anyone in the Sanhedrin, those throwing the stones, or Saul. The second insight—that Jesus was alive and that he was sharing in God's power and glory—was the incredible view of reality that infuriated the stoners and was likely the element Saul could not forget following the stoning.

Saul must have been troubled by the possibility that his concept of reality was flawed. Saul must have been theologically confident up until that moment, for until then he thought he understood the concepts of kingdom and power, good and evil. He was familiar with the Roman Empire and believed in the kingdom of God that the Messiah would one day establish. He understood the power of Rome, but believed in the power of God and its exercise within the framework of the covenant, the law, and the promises. He had grown up surrounded by the success of Rome in Tarsus, but believed in the triumph of the invisible God of his ancestors. What Saul believed about kingdom, power, control, good, and evil was shaken with the words of Stephen, who at his moment of death, glimpsed the living Lord of all. When Stephen saw the living Jesus triumphant in heaven, he was not afraid of Saul, the stoners, or of death itself.

It was in the context of cooperation between authorities of Rome and the Jewish temple that Jesus had been crucified, for he had threatened both. Saul of Tarsus, recognizing the ongoing and escalating attraction of Jesus' alternative version of the kingdom of God, was determined to help stamp out this threat to the restoration of Israel. But what was it about Jesus and his message of the kingdom of God that was distinctive, yet so attractive and threatening to both Rome and Saul?

We are now ready to look at Saul, who would take Jesus' message of the kingdom of God from the Sea of Galilee to the Mediterranean Sea. Peter's experience at Joppa and Caesarea was an invitation to accept the Roman invaders as humans created in God's image. But it was much more. It was an invitation for Peter to sail the pagan sea to the very heart of the power and the glory of the empire with the good news of the kingdom of God, the power of Jesus, and the glory of the crucified and living Lord of all.

It was Saul who would see the power of the living Jesus for himself on his terrorist mission en route to Damascus. This vision would change his life. It would also change history.

It was Paul who would continue to redefine Jesus' promises surrounded by promises of Rome. Paul, who would see the power of Rome with new eyes on his good news mission en route to the cities of the empire, would redefine the power of the cross. Paul would explore the Roman Empire and experiment with the good news of the kingdom of God, relating its promises of power and glory as an attractive alternative to the pagan promises of power and glory in the empire.

What kind of person was Saul at the time of conversion? Why did Jesus call the violent Saul to represent the kingdom in the empire? What did Paul learn about the nature of the precarious and powerful movement of the kingdom of God as he explored the reality of the Roman Empire?

4

Paul, the Seafaring Explorer of Empire

The Young Saul of Tarsus

FAR OFF THE BEATEN tourist track toward the northeastern corner of the Mediterranean Sea lies the rather nondescript city of Tarsus, Turkey. Once a bustling center of commerce, with the main east-west land route just to the north of the town, and a river harbor opening into the Mediterranean Sea on the south, there is not much to bring tourists here today. But our interest in Saul's early environment takes us to Tarsus.

Driving eastward across the vast expanses of Turkey, through Iconium (Konya today) and past the abandoned sites of Lystra and Derbe, surrounded by wheat fields, we approach the rugged Taurus mountain range, the great natural barrier between western and eastern Asia Minor. We wind laboriously upwards following overloaded trucks spewing diesel smoke, up the western side of the mountains, admiring the rugged beauty and fragrant pines. We are traveling the route of traders bringing silk from China, of Alexander the Great and his conquering armies, through the Cilician Gates, the narrow pass through which this ancient and modern road leads. Reaching the summit, we begin our descent behind trucks, now with squealing, overheated brakes, four thousand feet down to the Cilician Plains, toward the Mediterranean Sea, toward Tarsus.

As we reach the outskirts of Tarsus, the dust, potholes, and general scruffiness of this once important city helps to explain the absence of tourists. We seem to be the only travelers here today searching for remainders of Tarsus from the period of Saul's early life. Very few people we ask seem to know anything about Paul. Although the guidebook identifies Cleopatra's Gate, St. Paul's Well, and St. Paul's Church as having connections with Saul, these sites seem to have nothing to do with anything we have ever read in Acts. But still we try. We find the short stretch of excavated *cardo*, and imagine the boy Saul running past the columned shops lining the street. We visit the recently excavated Roman baths, which Saul's parents likely told their son to avoid. We even spot a tiny store selling snacks and water called "St. Paul's Glida." At least the memory of Paul has not entirely disappeared.

We return to the *cardo* and ponder this "no ordinary city" of Tarsus, the environment in which the young Saul was shaped. Was Saul, growing up here, an "ordinary" boy? Did growing up in Tarsus, a seaport at the northeast corner of the Mediterranean, instill in the young Saul the desire to see the world for himself?

While visiting Tarsus, I recalled an earlier conversation with Captain Steve, the retired Greek sea captain from whom we had purchased *SailingActs* in 2004 in our quest to sail the routes of Paul.

"Why are there so many Greek merchant ships and so many Greek captains in the shipping industry?" I asked after listening to his tales of life at sea one evening over dinner, and learning that, according to the captain, Greeks are the single largest ethnic group represented among the world's sea captains.

"We Greeks are adventurers, explorers," Captain Steve had explained with an air of self-satisfaction. "We like to explore the world. We like to explore the world of ideas as well. We are not afraid of new things."[1] This description certainly fit Captain Steve. I had been astonished earlier that evening with this seemingly unrefined sea captain's extensive library of philosophy and history, and his numerous paintings decorating his beautiful home.

---

1. The Greek openness to the world, others, and new ideas is one of the main points of Cahill's popular history of Greece, *Sailing the Wine Dark Sea*.

Does living on the edge of the sea shape one's attitude towards the world, especially the unknown parts? How much of the open-minded Greek view of the world did Saul the Jew absorb growing up in a seaport? Isn't it very likely that the young Saul met people whose stories of travel in far-off places and cultures fueled his curiosity about the world?

In Acts, Paul seems to display some of those distinctly Greek traits of curiosity, openness, adventure, and exploration by which he was surrounded growing up in Tarsus. Perhaps part of Paul's exasperation with his fellow Jewish believers later, especially those living in landlocked Jerusalem, was that they did not share his own traits of curiosity, openness, adventure, and exploration. We will look at Acts for insights into these possibilities about Paul.

Acts and the Dramatic Shift from Land to Sea

As mentioned in the previous chapter, the drama in Acts immediately begins to shift from the inland regions east of the shoreline of the Mediterranean to the sea and lands to the west around its rim. A cursory look at the maps in the back of many Bibles demonstrates this shift. In the entire Scriptures, the important port cities of Antioch and Caesarea are not mentioned until Acts. Joppa of the Jonah story is mentioned in the Old Testament only as a seaport and one of the several coastal cities that remained in enemy hands throughout most of Israel's history in Scripture, forcing the Israelites away from the coastline and into the hill country. Gaza, the Philistine city famous for Samson's undoing, is mentioned negatively a number of times in the Old Testament. But in the New Testament Gaza is mentioned in connection with the positive story of Philip and the Ethiopian official in Acts.

These four cities mentioned early in Acts, especially Antioch and Caesarea, are pivotal. Indeed Antioch and Caesarea, and to a lesser extent Joppa and Gaza, act as a kind of gigantic hinge of biblical, and eventually Western, history. Imagine an opened atlas of the biblical lands. The left page is blank, which seems to be a misprint. However, the right page is printed with a map of the biblical lands including the eastern end of the Mediterranean Sea with the port cities of Antioch, Caesarea, Joppa, and Gaza close to the left edge of the page, near the binding. Egypt is at the bottom left corner, and Haran, from where Abram is called south into the land he had been promised, is at the top in about the center of the page. The territory on the right page is all east of the shoreline of the Mediterranean, stretching to Babylon at the right edge of the map.

This is the map of the land stage on which the drama of God's actions among his people is performed—the Old Testament, the Gospels, and the first twelve chapters of Acts. All of the action, all of the writers, most of the readers, all of the places and people mentioned in Scripture up until the thirteenth chapter of Acts occurs on that page. There are only a few exceptions where the action strays from land to sea. Examples include Jonah's futile venture to escape God's attention by sailing westward on the Mediterranean, or descriptions and judgments against the people of the sea who continually threaten or upstage God's people of the land. Acts 1 through 12 takes the action irresistibly away from Jerusalem, the geographic and religious center of the land, and toward the seaports and the sea.

Now we turn the page to a new stage for the drama of God's action among his people. The back side of the Old Testament and Gospel's map is printed with the map of the action of God among his people from Acts 13 on. The left page is printed with the map and the right page is now blank. From Acts 13 until the final chapter in Revelation, the action is primarily the shoreline of Palestine and westward, on and around the Mediterranean Sea. All of the New Testament from Acts 13 on, with very few exceptions, was written about, from, to, and by people on and around the Mediterranean, all west of the shoreline of Palestine. In contrast to the map of the old world of the land, this map is of the new world of the sea in the biblical story.

As with the new world of Western history, it was the seafarers who were at the forefront of significant shifts of maps, history, perceptions, and cultures. Seafarers were the eyes and ears of the cultures from which they came, viewing the world for others, making irreversible contacts with strangers, introducing these strangers to the ideas and knowledge they had brought with them, and bringing back home the ideas and knowledge from those they had met. Ultimately, these seafaring explorers and traders provided those who sent them with cultural mirrors. This made it possible for the sending cultures to view themselves in new ways. The people living in the seaports of the Mediterranean were at the forefront of this kind of cultural exchange, for they were connected to the world by the sea.

Sociologist Rodney Stark describes the kinds of people who lived in and utilized the urban seaports of the empire around the Mediterranean Sea.[2] These great cities were centers of pluralism. Their inhabitants were open to trading goods and gods, ideas and idols with the rest of the world. It is no surprise to discover that urban seaports were among the earliest cities in which churches were established. Paul, like other seafarers, utilized the seaports and connected with people open to the world. Of the five bishoprics of the Byzantine church that eventually developed—Rome, Constantinople, Alexandria, Antioch, and Jerusalem—only Jerusalem was not a seaport.

Empires and Explorers in History

Let us look at the characteristics of explorers and their role in history just a bit more closely. Both biblical and world history describe the tendency of powerful and wealthy nations to dominate those areas of the world considered to be richer, weaker, emptier, strategic, or in some other ways desirable or advantageous to their own purposes. Often explorers were commissioned by the rich and powerful of these nations as the first step of their dominating or exploiting agenda. The explorers' sense of power, authority, and importance was directly connected to the status of the nation that sent them. While these explorers may have spent years away from their home culture, their sense of duty and the potential financial rewards and status elevation continued to sustain and motivate them amid incredible challenges and difficulties. While the explorers' sense of self-importance may not have made sense or have been accepted by the people of the regions they were exploring, this did not necessarily diminish their confidence. The great ones would continue their journey until they achieved their objectives, sometimes even unto death.

Explorers opened up new worlds. These worlds may have existed in the imagination or fears of the nations doing the sending, but not in

2. Stark, *Cities of God*. Stark correlates a number of variables. Of cities having a Christian church by AD 100, 64 percent were port cities, compared to 24 percent inland cities. See pp. 225–40.

their experience. The new world was only new for the explorer and those whom the explorer represented. For the inhabitants of the land or culture that the explorer visited, it was the explorer who was new. This encounter between old and new ensured that some kind of cultural exchange always occurred, usually with some tension and misunderstanding, and often with violence.

Explorers were frequently controversial in their own day and were often simultaneously vilified and honored, denounced and envied. They were not simply sent into the world to learn as neutral observers, but rather to learn in order to increase the power, wealth, and control of those who sent them, whether kings, patrons or pirates, traders or tyrants. Most explorers hoped to increase their own status as well. Explorers usually had both a personal and an official agenda.

Because of this, history has not always treated the great explorers kindly. The controversial heroes of one era can be reinterpreted as perpetuators of oppression and expansion of exploitation in another. Today, researchers of all types—historians, cultural anthropologists, sociologists, and even market researchers—generally see themselves as being superior to the old-fashioned explorers. But what is an anthropologist other than an explorer of culture with a specialized vocabulary and a personal and official agenda? The question is not which explorers have an agenda but, rather, which explorers have a genuinely good agenda for the people they encounter. Which explorers bring positive change, or contribute positively to inevitable social change in the long run?

Prior to the first century, travel on and around the Mediterranean Sea was not only difficult and uncomfortable, it was also dangerous. Early exploration in the Mediterranean was done by the Phoenicians, Greeks, and other seafarers for the purpose of colonization, conquest, or trade.[3] About the time of Jesus, a new category of travel was beginning to occur. Because of the decline of pirating due to the size and success of the Roman navy, the growth of sea trade, and the thousands of miles of good Roman roads linking the empire, early tourism was taking off in the first century and continued to thrive in the second.

3. See Casson, *Travel*. Pages 59–64 detail some of the ancient explorations chronicled by Herodotus and the exploits of Hanno of Carthage sailing beyond the Pillars of Hercules, the ancient name for the Straits of Gibraltar, down the cost of Africa around 500 BC.

> The Mediterranean world of the first two centuries AD ... was bigger than it had ever been before. So was the volume of movement. The roads and sea ways were now thronged with traders in larger numbers than the Greek world had ever known, with armies, bureaucrats, couriers of the government post, and just plain tourists, from the few who traveled far and wide to see the great sights to the thousands that left for nearby beaches and hills to escape the heat of the cities.[4]

People could now travel in relative safety and explore their own history, myths, and legends. The wealthy could afford some level of comfort by having a small army of slaves and attendants to provide them with their required amenities. The agenda of these first-century travelers was the exploration of tourists, traveling for personal enjoyment and learning. Paul was different.

Paul the Explorer

What the great seafaring explorers in history did for the world, Paul did for the Christian movement of the West and, because of that, for Western history. Paul can be understood as an explorer of the dynamic pagan culture of the Roman Empire around the rim of the Mediterranean Sea. Paul's understanding of the kingdom of God and the lordship of Jesus was expanded and refined during his exploration of the success and scope of the Roman Empire and the power of the Caesar. Recognizing and appreciating this feature of Paul's life gives insight into and appreciation for the way Paul's mission activity and theology developed in his travels in the Roman Empire. Let's examine this characterization a bit further.

Although travel was increasing in the first century, "most citizens, other than merchants and soldiers, did not travel much; Paul's extensive travels were quite unusual."[5] Paul was likely one of the most well traveled of his class in the first century. But it is not merely the extent of his journeys that make him an explorer, but rather the nature of his journeys and his unique agenda related to his vision of Jesus and the kingdom of God. Only when he lingered to work and organize a church, or during

---

4. Ibid., 127. See also Perrottet, *Pagan Holiday*, 3–7.

5. Jeffers, *Greco-Roman World*, 202.

the winter months when travel was restricted by weather, or when he was prevented by imprisonment, was Paul kept in one place for very long over a period of ten to twelve years. Only prison or death, it seemed, would keep Paul from moving ever farther from Jerusalem.

Was Paul an explorer by nature and experience as a youth in Tarsus? Did this change with his encounter with Jesus on the road to Damascus? If so, how?

We look again at Saul growing up in Tarsus. There the young Saul would have certainly observed the "ends of the earth" passing through by land and sea. As was mentioned earlier, Tarsus was not only a seaport, but was on the main route running from east to west, and stood at the entrance of the Cilician Gates. The rugged range of the Taurus Mountains, with the distinct pass of the Cilician Gates, is visible from Tarsus. These gates, like the seaport to the Mediterranean on the Cydnus River, would have fueled the imagination of a curious, energetic, and clever boy like Saul. What is the world like beyond the Gates, beyond the horizon? Saul grew up observing the exotic parade of cultures, languages, and religions passing through Tarsus.

His travel at a young age to study in Jerusalem, the place of pilgrimage for Jews scattered throughout the whole of the Roman Empire, would have added to his understanding and curiosity. For as his commitment to Judaism grew, his awareness of the attractive and threatening power and triumph of Rome would have also increased. According to William Ramsey, Saul "had been brought up from infancy in the Greek city of Tarsus as at once a citizen of that city and also a citizen of the imperial city of Rome. He had been trained to a far wider outlook on the world than the people of Jerusalem could attain to. He knew the pagan world from inside, its needs, its desires, its religious longings, its weakness, and its crimes."[6]

Saul's early travels following his education in Jerusalem appear to be motivated by a reactionary agenda, an attempt to prevent the erosion of religious tradition and the relentless temptation of Hellenism for the Jews to participate in the seductive power and share the glory of pagan Rome. The persecution of the Christians may have been in part a misguided defense against the inroads of Hellenism, laxity, and especially disunity within the Jewish community that Saul perceived was being fostered by

6. Ramsay, *St. Paul*, 45.

the followers of Jesus. Jewish identity was immensely important for Saul, a Roman citizen coming from Tarsus. Ramsey describes the special rights and privileges that the Jewish community of Tarsus enjoyed,[7] and Saul most likely had observed the erosion of Jewish identity among those who enjoyed such benefits of the Roman system.

Saul's curiosity and fascination with the world and its people coupled with his religious passion is evident prior to his conversion. As noted earlier, Saul displayed curiosity at Stephan's execution and seems to have listened carefully to Stephan's final vision of Jesus recorded in Acts (7:54—8:1).

His rampage toward Damascus, at his own initiative but backed by the religious authorities in Jerusalem, is also indicative of his character. Damascus was technically outside of the jurisdiction of Rome at that time, and it is unclear whether Jewish religious authority legally extended to Damascus. We see a quality of Saul that we will observe latter in his mission activities—he operates on the margins, pushes the boundaries, takes risks, and explains later. This is a pattern of many explorers in history.

Saul's encounter with Jesus does not change Paul's character and his pattern of operation. Jesus begins Saul's new agenda by giving him open-ended directions. Through a vision to Ananias, Saul was commissioned as Jesus' "instrument whom I have chosen to carry my name before the Gentiles and kings and before the people of Israel" (Acts 9:15). While this new commission certainly changed Saul's itinerary, it did not slow his previous momentum. No one, not even the Jewish authorities in Jerusalem, the Romans, the cautious leaders of the church in Jerusalem, or rioting pagans, could restrict Saul now. Antioch would send him off into the empire with Barnabas, but it was the commissioning of Jesus that gave Saul the dangerous and productive confidence that would mark his travels.

A *Guidebook of Greece*, written by Pausanias sometime between AD 160 and 180, is the only surviving travel guide from ancient times. The recommended itinerary, however, "did not venture further west than Italy; after all, a typical ancient tourist, principally interested in monuments of the hoary past, would find little to engage his attention in the relatively new centers that had sprung up in the wake of Rome's conquest of Gaul,

7. Ibid., 36–37.

Spain, and Britain."[8] Contrast this to Paul, who indicated his desire to go to Spain and beyond. Paul was no mere tourist!

As with other explorers, Paul's itinerary was open-ended and ever expanding as he learned of other places through the stories he heard aboard ships and from itinerant people he met along the way. There are hints of this in the Acts story, such as the dream of the man from Macedonia pleading with Paul to come there and help. Dreams, visions, the Holy Spirit, all are given credit for extending and modifying Paul's already ambitious travel plans. One can be sure, as dreams tend to follow deeply held desires, that Paul was completely willing to cooperate with his heavenly visitors and comply with their instructions to go farther. Why did he never dream of or receive special instructions to stay home?

Roland Allen and others since have attempted with a great deal of insight to summarize "Paul's missionary methods."[9] Paul's strategy, Allen and others have concluded, was to select key urban centers, administrative centers with flourishing seaports and/or on major transportation routes, and there establish a church. The gospel then would expand outward naturally from this center into the surrounding cities and territory. This is a logical and useful way of making sense of Paul's itineraries.

But there is other evidence that does not quite fit this overall strategy. Paul goes alone and explores the legendary city of Athens, preaches only briefly, then continues on to Corinth, another city famously attractive to the ancient travelers with its wealth, license, pleasure, and success. Is it not a strong possibility that Paul was visiting these centers of pagan culture in order to understand their good and evil, their attraction, their promises, and their power and triumph in light of his vision of Jesus on the road to Damascus? This understanding is consistent with Paul's desire to go to Rome, a place where the church already existed, and to Spain where Christians already lived.

But did Paul understand himself as an explorer? Didn't he talk about his motivations for travel in the Roman Empire only in terms of preaching the gospel and visiting Christian communities in distant places? Or are both exploration and mission two features of the same endeavor for Paul,

---

8. Casson. *Travel*, 294.

9. Allen, *Missionary Methods*.

seeking to communicate the good news of Jesus and the kingdom of God to the pagans of the Roman Empire? What kind of explorer was Paul?

Paul, Flexible Explorer with a Clear Agenda

Paul was an explorer capable of changing his presuppositions. Paul's mission voyages were filled with the risks of personal change, risks typical of explorers on extended voyages away from their home cultures. Explorers not only take physical and emotional risks as they push into unfamiliar, unpredictable, and sometimes dangerous territory, they take the risk that their perceptions of others and themselves will be dramatically changed in the process. For Saul the most dramatic change in his understanding of Jesus occurred when they met on the way to Damascus. It is no accident that this change occurred on a journey, on another occasion when Saul was pushing out beyond the limits of legitimacy.

Following this conversion, change continued but more gradually. As Paul traveled, surrounded by pagans on whom he relied during the storms, the shipwrecks, and other challenges of the sea, it seems that his attitude toward them began to soften as he benefited from their skills, their gifts, their qualities of openness, and their friendship. This is the risk of explorers who are vulnerable and dependent on the very people they may have once mistrusted and feared, or regarded as dangerous and evil. They begin to view the world, themselves, and their own background from the strangers' perspectives.

The risk of misunderstanding when the explorer returns back home is predictable. The explorer has survived with the help of strangers whom the home culture continues to misunderstand, fear, and even hate. Those who have not experienced the goodness of their enemies will not understand those who have. This is perhaps the most problematic for Paul in attempting to relate to the brothers in Jerusalem. How can he get the landlocked and defensive believing Jews of Jerusalem to accept the open-minded believing people of the great Mediterranean port cities whom he has come to know, appreciate, admire, and respect?

Paul was ready to take relational risks in order to complete his goals. Explorers face the risk of abandonment or worse from those who join the expedition. On the first recorded mission voyage in Acts 13, John Mark starts out with Saul and Barnabas, likely traveling by sea for the first time in his life from Antioch to Salamis, Cyprus. It is likely that John Mark experiences a kind of cultural shock on the overnight voyage on a pagan vessel. While the pagan power and triumph of Rome on display in Salamis, their port of arrival on the island, was similar to that of Antioch, as Paul, Barnabas, and John Mark make their way overland, John Mark was likely observing with growing alarm the change in Paul's attitudes toward Gentiles.

By the time they arrive in Paphos on the western end of Cyprus far from Antioch now, and after Sergius Paulus, the Roman proconsul of Cyprus became a believer, John Mark notices that Saul even begins to use his Roman name, Paulus, exclusively. There in Paphos, in the very heart of the island's renowned Aphrodite worship, John Mark observes the eager male pilgrims flocking to visit the sites connected to the beautiful goddess of love. Finally he takes what will be for him the final leg of the voyage, from Cyprus to Perge, Pamphilia (modern Turkey). This is another overnight voyage on a pagan ship, farther from home physically and spiritually than John Mark has ever been. Paul is getting too close, much too close, to the pagans. If these pagans can influence Paul's itinerary, what else might Paul be willing to change?[10]

By the time the small band of sailors dock in the harbor of the magnificent and thoroughly pagan Perge, John Mark is probably experiencing not only a cultural shock, but a theological shock as well. He is not suffering from seasickness or any other kind of physical affliction, or he would not have returned immediately the same way he came. He cannot go farther. Openness to the strange and threatening world is not easy to accept in your leader unless one shares the same trait. John Mark, it seems, did not. He could no longer completely trust Paul and Barnabas although he likely finds some sympathy from the latter. He could no longer talk to Paul without an argument. As for Paul, he neither deviated from his own plans

10. There is some speculation that the missionary band was originally intending to go to Alexandria, Egypt, from Cyprus. There is also evidence that Sergius Paulus had connections in Pisidian Antioch and had persuaded Paul to go to that inland city instead, a very unusual choice that does not fit the later pattern of Paul's preference of port cities. Pisidian Antioch demonstrates the high level of resistance typical of the more conservative inland cities. Additionally, when the missionary band arrives in the port city of Perge, a very logical place for Paul to preach, Paul and Barnabas continue on immediately to Antioch over the rugged Taurus Mountains, a long and difficult journey by foot.

nor seemed to worry about John Mark returning alone, even though he knew that John Mark would defend his decision to abandon the journey by criticizing Paul to the sending church in Antioch.

Loneliness is part of the life of an explorer. While Paul certainly made friends—and enemies—wherever he went, and while he usually traveled and labored with very close companions, both men and women, this kind of exploration is a lonely journey at times. It is debated whether Paul was married. While it would have conceivably been possible for Paul to have been married and sustained his lifestyle of exploration, it makes little difference in his experience of loneliness. Whether or not he had a wife, it is clear that he did not see much of her. Paul's friendships and close working relationships with a variety of others were durable, but never continuous. Paul's letters and the dramatic farewell scenes recorded in Acts give clues to the pain of separation and loneliness Paul endured.

Paul was physically and mentally tough. Paul experienced and described the physical hardships of first century travel. Paul walked many hundreds of miles through rugged, sun-scorched terrain.[11] He experienced dangers from both natural and human sources. Acts and portions of the Epistles contain an amazing catalogue of detailed hardship stories, forming some of the most reliable descriptions of travel conditions contained in first-century historical documents.

Paul is not only aware of this, he writes, as explorers do, about the hardships he endures. In his letter to the people in Corinth, who themselves are very familiar with the human and natural hazards of life and travel, Paul writes, "To the present hour we go hungry and thirsty, we are poorly clothed and beaten and homeless" (1 Cor 4:11). In case the people of Corinth need reminding, in his second letter Paul catalogues the list in a new way:

> [I have had] far greater labors, far more imprisonments, with countless floggings, and often near death. Five times I received from the Jews the forty lashes minus one. Three times I was beaten

---

11. You can actually hike parts of Paul's first route to get a feel for the stamina and perseverance of Paul beginning with that first journey. A new trail called the St. Paul Trail, linking Perge with Antioch, has been recently developed. Kate Clow, the developer of the trail, in her trail guidebook *St. Paul Trail* estimates that it takes about five weeks to complete the route between Perge and Antioch. That is only a small part of the overland travel Paul did on his first journey!

> with rods. Once I received a stoning. Three times I was ship-
> wrecked; for a night and day I was adrift at sea; on frequent jour-
> neys, in danger from rivers, danger from bandits, danger from my
> own people, danger from Gentiles, danger in the city, in danger in
> the wilderness, danger at sea, in danger from false brothers and
> sisters; in toil and hardship, through many a sleepless night, hun-
> gry and thirsty, often without food, cold and naked. And, besides
> other things, I am under daily pressure because of my anxiety for
> all the churches. (2 Cor 11:23–28)

This indicates both the conditions of sea travel and the amount of travel Paul undertook. Few people besides sailors had this much experience of sea travel in the first century. The credentials of explorers are established in their tales of hardships they have endured. The "boasting" that Paul does about these travel hardships on land and sea is the kind of thing that explorers and other adventurers do. What is avoided by most people is cited by Paul as a badge of honor, something that explorers tend to do in order to impress others, especially when others have credentials of higher social standing. Paul seems to be emulating Jesus, who once reminded would-be followers of higher status that "Foxes have holes, and the birds of the air have nests; but the Son of Man has nowhere place to lay his head" (Luke 9:58).

Paul, like other of Jesus' followers, also gloried in the crucifixion of Jesus. What is shame for most Roman citizens is glory for Jesus' followers. These are the credentials of the outsider, the marginalized, the innovator, the entrepreneur, and the adventurer. Christianity, before it became legal and official, was founded and accepted by such people and became the kind of movement that attracted them.

Paul was an explorer of the Roman Empire with a vision of the kingdom of God. Paul's exploratory travels continuously expanded his awareness of the nature of the pagan Roman Empire. Following his encounter with Jesus on the Damascus road, whatever view Saul the Pharisee had of the empire was modified by his understanding of the kingdom of God as he recognized the reality of the living Jesus. And it was in the context of examining the scope and success of the Roman Empire that Paul's vision of the kingdom expanded and matured.

Paul continuously compared and contrasted his observations and intense experiences in the Roman Empire with his own experiences and observations as a visionary follower of Jesus. His time among people, his conversations, his keen observations, and his depth of passion as he contemplated the strengths and weakness of the world in which he was moving, is indication that he was a keen explorer with an alternative vision.

On the ship voyages, through those long passages with little wind, or during times spent waiting in port for the ship's cargo to be loaded, Paul had time to ponder and reflect on the competing realities and promises of the Roman Empire and the kingdom of God defined by Jesus. Each port city on the Mediterranean flaunted the successes of the political and religious system of the empire. Paul constantly overheard the tales of religious pilgrims, complete with graphic detail of the pleasures of Aphrodite and licentiousness of Dionysus, in the conversations of pagan sailors, soldiers, and travelers in seaports and on ship decks.

Then the wind picks up or the mob threatens and Paul experiences the protection of these pagans, the sailors, the soldiers, and fellow travelers. Once again he recognizes that pagans too are created in the image of God and may be far closer to Jesus and his kingdom than he himself once was. At times Paul experiences the disdain from these people, their ridicule, their power to punish and imprison. Other times he receives their generosity, protection, and affirmation. Paul becomes an expert of pagan culture and thought on those long voyages. He understands experientially the good and evil of the pagan world.

For a period of at least ten years, the growing perception of the power and triumph of the Roman Empire is informed by a corresponding expansion of the vision and anticipation of the power and triumph of the kingdom of God. Paul's experience with the authority of Rome is evaluated and challenged by his growing understanding of authority of Jesus. Paul's exploration has features of military reconnaissance, for Paul is exploring not only the strengths, but the weaknesses and vulnerability of the mighty empire in light of his vision of Jesus and the coming kingdom.

Paul, who once was completely committed to recovering fidelity to the Torah and had longed for the restoration of the kingdom of Israel, was surrounded by the reality of the most powerful empire the world had ever known. In Paul's mission-oriented exploration of the Roman Empire he must have become increasingly aware that even the high points of the Israelite kingdom under David and Solomon were relatively insignificant in comparison to the power and glory of the Roman Empire. The futility of resistance or violent revolution must have been increasingly clear as he sailed the Mediterranean. Paul's conviction of the triumph of Jesus over all previous and current empires of death and enslavement continued to grow.

Paul's exploration is shaped by his confidence of the power and authority of the resurrected Jesus and the implications for everyone in the empire, regardless of status, ethnicity, gender, or heritage. While Greek was the *lingua franca* of the empire, and Latin was the official political language, a variety of languages and dialects were spoken throughout the empire. There was a vast array of religious and mythical identities as well. The Roman Empire was amazingly diverse and pluralistic in every sense. While Paul would have been acquainted with this pluralism, he had not developed cultural and theological insights into this diversity until he experienced the empire and its peoples for extended periods of time as a Christian. Jesus' kingdom, in Paul's imagination, would surpass the ability of the Roman Empire to incorporate the grand diversity of the human family into a unified family of God.

Paul was motivated by an agenda to connect the good news of the kingdom to the triumphs and failures of Rome experienced by the people of the empire. In his travels Paul came to conclusions about the strengths and the weaknesses of the empire's system based on the vision of the reality of the living Jesus. The growing awareness of the universal applicability and the goodness of the gospel in the flawed and failing Roman Empire motivated and inspired Paul to move on to new places, rather than to remain too long in one place building the church. He was not content to repeat the introduction of the gospel in familiar contexts only, but he wanted to try increasingly challenging cities such as Rome and beyond.

Paul was an explorer with an agenda of change. He traveled the empire on land and sea with the life-changing, life-giving message of Jesus and the kingdom of God. Is this kind of exploration not at the heart of the story of God's people moving in the world, blessing others and being blessed in the process? Is not this kind of exploration at the center of the faithful representation of the good news of the kingdom of God in the pagan world empire of Western globalization? If we understand Paul this way, we have a model for Christians in globalization that calls for ongoing, rigorous cultural exploration done with a vision of Jesus and an agenda of sharing the good news.

However, Paul was more than an explorer with a vision and an agenda. He was an entrepreneur of the good news of the risen Lord Jesus and the coming kingdom within the reality of the powerful and glorious Roman Empire. It is this entrepreneurial feature of Paul's exploration that offers twenty-first-century Christians an additional model of faithful, relevant engagement with the globalized world of the future.

5

Paul, Entrepreneur
of the Kingdom in Empire

You can easily drive from Tarsus to Syrian Antioch (modern Antakya, Turkey) in a matter of hours following the modern roads around the northeast corner of the Mediterranean. If you are vigilant as you drive toward the center of the sprawling city of Antioch, you can spot the small signs directing you toward St. Peter's Church on the outskirts, up on the slope of the hills surrounding the city built on the banks of the Orontes River. This old cave-chapel is the very place in which, according to the tradition, the early church met and where it is thought that Peter preached during his visit to Antioch (Gal 2:11).

Although the entrance fee seems a little expensive for the chance to look inside the dark little cave, it is well worth it. For here, away from the noise, heat, and congestion of modern Antakya, you have time to contemplate the dynamic, creative, pioneering congregation that launched a deliberate mission movement from here that would spread throughout the Roman Empire.

Located in a major seaport, the congregation had regular visitors from Cyprus and other Mediterranean ports, Jews and gentile proselytes worshiping together, and refugees escaping persecution in Jerusalem. We remember that "in the church at Antioch there were prophets and teachers: Barnabas, Simeon who was called Niger, Lucius of Cyrene,

Manaen a member of the court of Herod the ruler and Saul" (Acts 13:1). What an interesting collection of humanity in that single congregation in Antioch! What would it have been like to be in that ethnically, socially, and economically diverse and creative group? Did those people others called "Christians" have any idea what they were doing when they commissioned and sent away Saul, Barnabas, and John Mark to take the gospel west toward Cyprus and beyond?

After leaving the cave, you visit the museum along the Orontes River containing magnificent displays of exquisite mosaics that demonstrate the wealth and beauty of Antioch at the time of the early congregation described in Acts. There are a number of pagan gods as well on display in the museum. The image of one, dating to 100 BC, is called the "river god." The Christians of Antioch, the first place in the world where the followers of Jesus were so labeled, would have worshipped Jesus surrounded by these gods who had obviously blessed Antioch with life-giving water, with power, and with success. Antioch was in the high-status league of Rome and Alexandria.

You drive out to explore Antioch's harbor in Seleucia, almost twenty miles away, where the Orontes River empties into the Mediterranean. You wind your way out of Antioch toward the coast without getting too lost, then turn north for a few miles to the fishing harbor and find the old rock jetty of the ancient harbor in the water. You can climb up one of the cliffs where the ruins of a Doric temple to Zeus once dominated the high area around the harbor.

When Saul and the others looked back toward Antioch on that first journey they would have seen the temple to Zeus long after the waving Christians in the harbor had disappeared. Saul turns and looks ahead toward Cyprus, just over the horizon. His ten-year voyage of exploration and experimentation, which will change him, the Christian movement, and world history, has begun. Saul is leaving Antioch and will return as Paul.

Paul's Public Experiment of God's Promises

To view Paul as an experimenter with the good news of the kingdom of God within the Roman Empire may seem at first to give the impression that Paul is being conceptualized as "neutral" or "objective," in the way that modern social scientists believe themselves to be, or at least attempt to be. Nothing could be farther from truth with Paul. He was biased and subjective. His quest was to connect the good news of the kingdom of God to the experiences and understanding of the variety of the empire's inhabitants who were shaped by Rome's system of good and evil and surrounded by its power and success. This quest made him a central part of the experiment. Paul was himself, in a sense, the object of experimentation. He was the test case for the good news of the kingdom in the Roman Empire.

As Paul explored the good and evil, the power, domination, and triumph of the Roman Empire, he experimented with the gospel on two levels. On one level he was experimenting with ways of understanding and applying the theological content of the gospel both within and outside of the framework of Jewish understandings. Concepts such as "salvation," "faith," "kingdom," and "power" were reframed, redefined, developed, and expanded by Paul in relation to his personal realization and appropriation of the gospel during his experience of making the good news of the kingdom known throughout the empire.

A second level of experimentation had to do with the propagation and communication of these concepts within the pagan culture. Paul was continually attempting to make connections between the pagan ideals, practices, cultural patterns, experiences, hopes, and dreams with those of the gospel. These two levels of personal and public experimentation could be seen as following the precedent of biblical heroes of faith such as Abraham, whose life of faith was a lifelong, personal experiment with the promises of God, and a public demonstration of the results as they occurred.

Jesus had commissioned and sent his apostles as witnesses in "Jerusalem, Judea, Samaria, ends of the earth" (Acts 1:8). They had a lot to learn, for none of the places mentioned by Jesus in the commissioning were familiar to the Galilean disciples. The cultural distance between the Galileans and the urban dwellers of Jerusalem, especially the religious and social elite, was immense. Judea was also unfamiliar territory for the apostles, while Samaria and the "ends of the earth" were in many ways completely foreign cultures. For the followers of Jesus, all of the places

Jesus mentioned, even Jerusalem, needed to be explored with the new perception of the kingdom of God. The apostles needed to explore their world and experiment with the gospel in each place mentioned by Jesus in order to carry out the mandate of Jesus to be his witnesses.

With the persecution of the church described in Acts 11:19–21, the followers of Jesus living in and around Jerusalem were scattered and took refuge in many places around the Mediterranean Sea, including the city of Antioch. In that wealthy, tolerant, open, pagan port city, the church obviously thrived. The experimentation that had begun within the Jewish community in Jerusalem began to expand into the pagan world. The remarkable story of the complaint of the Hellenized widows and the response of the congregation recounted in Acts 6:1–7 demonstrates that this was a new situation. The solution was an experiment that proved to be viable. The challenge, the process of deciding what to try, and the effects of their innovation are all part of the sacred story. Trying things for the first time, or experimentation, is the norm for authentic witness in Acts as in much of the rest of Scripture.

The Christians of Antioch however, were radically different from those of Jerusalem. These were urban opportunists, people from all parts of the empire around the Mediterranean who were attracted to Antioch for reasons of pleasure and profit, religion and refuge. Saul, from both Tarsus and Jerusalem, likely felt quite at home when he arrived there. He would have learned from this amazing variety of people, and contributed his own energy and creativity to the ethos of the congregation. It was in this congregation in Antioch where Saul's creation-formed and exodus-based understanding of the Roman Empire and the kingdom of God defined by Jesus must have been fundamentally shaped in a way that took him with confidence through the empire with the gospel.

Saul likely participated in the Antioch congregation's decision to send him and Barnabas on their initial mission journey. This journey was the initial exploration of deliberate expansion westward, the primary experiment that would shape not only the direction of Paul's life until it ended in Rome, but the westward expansion of the Christian movement in the Roman Empire. What had begun in Galilee would become a universal faith, and the decision of the congregation to send Saul and Barnabas on their journey was a major experiment. It was a risk with no certain outcome. Had it not succeeded, we would not know about it.

While the congregation in Antioch commissioned and organized this great mission of exploration and experimentation, it was Paul who personally embodied the feature of experimentation with the gospel throughout the ethnic and religious pluralism of the Roman Empire. Acts is filled with evidence that depicts Paul as an experimenter; Paul's reflections from his activities in the Epistles reinforce this picture.

Before we look at the evidence, some general points about the nature of Paul's experimentation need to be clarified. Paul was not experimenting about whether to make Christ known, but how. He was not seeking to determine whether the gospel was true and powerful; he was experimenting with ways to demonstrate the gospel's truth and power within the deceit and power of the Roman Empire with its persuasive display of the apparent validity of pagan promises. He was not experimenting with whether Jesus' power and glory could compete with Rome's; he was experimenting with how to make that vision credible to those surrounded by the hard evidence of Rome's power and glory.

In a general sense, Paul's life demonstrates the missional nature of biblical faith—a lifelong personal experiment of obedience to God, performed in public, that demonstrates to one's own satisfaction, and sometimes to the satisfaction of others, the credibility of God's promises. The exigencies of life, the challenges, the distractions of the responsibilities of living, the temptations to believe the definitions and promises of good of the world's systems and its rewards, the suffering and struggle with the evil of the world's systems, all are part of the context in which the experiment of faith is conducted. Abraham, Moses, and the heroes of faith in the Hebrew scriptures all demonstrated that the world is a public laboratory of faith, a stage on which the believers of God's promises perform their faith in them.

Even faith in the resurrection is a high-risk experiment that is sometimes witnessed by the public. Jesus' crucifixion and Stephan's stoning are examples of this dramatic display of faith in public, as are many deaths of martyrs through the ages. Jesus' faith was necessary for him to face his own death rather than to seek to preserve his life. While Jesus' resurrection demonstrates the validity of believing Jesus' promise of resurrection for his followers, death is a personal test of the validity of that claim, a final experiment in a life shaped and sustained by the promise of the resurrection.

We are not simply talking here about learning through the experience of surviving and coping in the world as a believer in Jesus. Paul's model, rather, is about learning through deliberate attempts to experiment, to try out the gospel in relation to the various human alternatives, to continuously seek to connect the future vision and present reality of the kingdom with the reality and aspirations of the world. This makes experimentation bold and proactive, rather than desperate and defensive. The story in Acts depicts Paul as continuously taking risks in order to test the possibilities of making the good news known and credible to others, rather than avoiding risks in order to experience personal benefits and blessings of faith.

Paul did not attempt to learn about the power of the gospel in the context of the power of Rome by observing others trying it out. Paul's life of faith was an experiment in which he himself took the risks. The suffering and the hardships Paul endured are both the risk of the experiment and the validation of the premise. This is in marked contrast to much of today's popular Christian literature with its advice on how to take the risk out of faith, how to make living in the world predictable and tame. These popular Christian promises of success and rewards are remarkably similar to the pagan promises within the surrounding culture. Paul never seems to be used in this literature as a model for this safe, secure, and selfish kind of faith.

Paul, the Entrepreneur

Paul, the Jew and Roman citizen, can also be understood as an entrepreneur of the gospel within the Roman Empire. His theology of the new identity of the believers in Jesus was deeply personal, for it grew directly out of his experiences as both a Jew and a Roman citizen. It grew out of his efforts of including Gentiles fully in the promises of the kingdom. His growing concern, and eventually his primary preoccupation with attempting to bring Jews and Greeks together with a new identity through common faith in Jesus, was a part of Paul's visionary innovation and application of the gospel of the kingdom in the Roman Empire.

I recall a conversation with a young Israeli customs official when we arrived on *SailingActs* in Ashkelon, Israel, at the end of our first sailing season in 2004. During his inspection of the boat he had noticed the icon of St. Paul hanging in the salon. "Who is that?" he had asked.

"The Apostle Paul."

"Why do you have a picture of him on your boat?"

"We're following his travels," I had replied. "He was Jewish, and had studied in Jerusalem before becoming a follower of Jesus."

"What did Paul do that made him special," the customs officer asked.

After pondering this unusual question from a customs officer I had answered, "Well, I think his biggest contribution was his efforts to get the Jewish believers in Jesus to accept Greek pagan believers in Jesus into their churches," I explained. "This is what makes him controversial."

"Why would that be controversial?" the customs officer had asked. "That sounds like a good idea to me." I had agreed, but did not mention to the Israeli officer that Paul's position was as inflammatory then as it would be for someone today to make the case for an unrestricted welcome and full inclusion of all Palestinians into the Jewish state of Israel.

This example is but one of a number of highly original and personally risky innovations with the gospel in the Roman Empire in which Paul participated during his years of constant travel and labor. The following examples are not exhaustive, but demonstrate some of the unique and original interpretations and applications of the message of the gospel in the life of Paul in the empire. Some of these examples are detailed only in the Acts story. While it is customary to study Paul's conclusions in his Epistles about what he learned through his innovations, the record in Acts allows us to observe the process prior to his conclusions. Perhaps the experimental method of Paul is as informative to contemporary Christians as are Paul's conclusions. Let us examine several important innovations.

Jewish and non-Jewish identity. Within the pagan Roman Empire, religious differences were almost irrelevant as long as the divinity of the emperors was not threatened.[1] From the point of view of Rome's policy of toleration of religious pluralism, the monotheistic Jews, who stubbornly

1. Jeffers, *Greco-Roman World*, 105; Crossan and Reed, *In Search of Paul*, 4.

refused to acknowledge the validity of both the pagan gods and the divinity of the emperor, posed a threat to the empire's agenda of integration and unity. Due to their sheer numbers[2] throughout the empire and their stubbornness in resisting integration into the imperial cult, which Rome used elsewhere to ensure the integration of its subjects, Jews were a distinct but specially tolerated part of the Roman system. The compromise on the side of the Jews implicit in this arrangement was very likely one of the motivations for religious zealots like Saul in persecuting the early followers of Jesus. He would have perceived the gospel's early attraction to the Hellenized Jews and gentile God-fearers and proselytes as a potentially dangerous breakdown of the distinct identity that protected the Jewish community from the drift toward compromise with the surrounding pagan culture.

With his encounter with Jesus on the Damascus road, Saul's perception of Jesus was not only radically converted, but his perception of Jesus' followers, which included Hellenized Jews and gentile God-fearers and proselytes, was converted as well. Following his conversion, immersed in the strange new world of the early church community, with time spent exploring beyond the margins of the empire (Arabia) and especially in the dynamic inclusive congregation in Antioch, Saul was exposed to a new form of identity that was neither pagan Hellenistic nor religiously Jewish. This identity did not fit the good/evil categories of either the Roman pagan system or Judaism but was based on the reality Saul observed and experienced among those who followed Jesus.

Paul's famous statement in his first letter to the Corinthians gives evidence of his personal innovation with ethnic and religious identity. "To the Jews I became as a Jew, in order to win the Jews. . . . To those outside the law I became as one outside the law . . . so that I might win those outside the law. . . . I have become all things to all people that I might by all means save some. I do it all for the sake of the gospel, so that I may share in its blessings" (1 Cor 9:20–23). This statement is remarkably bold even

2. "By the time of Christ, Jews were widely dispersed throughout the cities and countryside of the Empire and beyond. . . . In New Testament times, only about 2.5 million Jews lived in Palestine, while 4 to 6 million lived outside of Palestine. . . . There was a substantial Jewish population in virtually every town of any decent size in the Mediterranean region" (Jeffers, *Greco-Roman World*, 213). Some scholars estimate the Jewish population within the Roman Empire to be as high as 10 percent.

today, but in the first-century Roman Empire it was a revolutionary and dangerous personal experiment of social and religious sabotage.

In Paphos, Cyprus, at the beginning of his first mission journey recorded in Acts, several key innovative shifts occur. First, Saul proclaims the gospel to Sergius Paulus, the proconsul of Cyprus who, incredibly, believes; second, Saul is referred to as "Paul" from that point on in the Acts story. This event prepares for and lies behind Paul's announcement in the next major place of witness, Pisidian Antioch, following resistance from the Jewish community, that he is now "turning to the Gentiles" (13:46). Let us consider the evidence that both of these developments were deliberate personal experiments with the gospel in the context of the dynamic tension between of the attraction of Hellenism and the resistant exclusivism of the Jewish communities within the empire.

First, there was an innovative identity shift in the name change. Saul, like most Jews in the eastern Mediterranean, was known by his Hebrew name within the Jewish community. Because Saul's father was a Roman citizen, Saul had a Latin name as well. "*Paulus* would have been the *cognomen* of Paul's citizen name" and "was probably chosen by his parents as the closest Latin equivalent to the Hebrew Saul."[3] Luke uses "Saul," the Hebrew name, exclusively up until Paphos, and from then on only "Paul."

This almost-unnoticed name shift is mentioned in the context of the intense, brief story of Barnabas and Saul being summoned by Sergius Paulus for a hearing and the attempt by Elymas the sorcerer to oppose the message and prevent his employer from believing, Saul's rebuttal and Elymas's instant blindness, and finally Sergius Paulus's acceptance of the gospel. Only seven action-packed verses give the details (13:6–12), but knowing the context of the story deepens the drama. At the time of Barnabas and Saul's visit, Cyprus was a Mediterranean center of Aphrodite worship, with Paphos the capital city of that center. According to the legend, just a few miles south of Paphos was the place where Aphrodite stepped ashore after emerging out of the sea foam. Close to this site the great temple to Aphrodite had been constructed. The place where Aphrodite is said to have bathed was just north of Paphos. All sites connected to Aphrodite

---

3. Ibid., 205. See pp. 202–6 for a discussion of the complex and changing system of male names (*nomen, praenomen, cognomen*) in the Roman Empire in the first century connected to citizenship, social status, and identity.

attracted droves of devotees from all over the Mediterranean at the time of Saul's visit.

Saul and Barnabas came to Paphos after preaching throughout Cyprus, to the very place that was permeated with Aphrodite worship and most likely humming with visitors on pilgrimage. Paul's very first known gentile convert, Sergius Paulus, was the highest official of Cyprus, the proconsul. Was Saul, "also known as Paul," simply becoming Hellenized? Hardly! Although John Mark may have viewed this move with some suspicion and concern, Paul was attempting new ways of identifying with all potential followers of Jesus, both Jew and Greek, within the politically united but socially divided empire.

There is another significant change in the name pattern contained in the story. Up until Paphos in the narrative, Luke has referred to the leaders of the mission team as "Barnabas and Saul." From now on he will refer to them as "Paul and Barnabas." In the story, the success of Saul the follower resulted in Paul the leader, a literary pattern Luke follows consistently in Acts regardless of who joins the mission team. "In Christ, we are a new creation," Paul would later write. "Everything has become new!" (2 Cor 5:17). This conclusion is likely directly related to Paul's own experiment with his changing identity.

The second experiment that seems to be related to Paul's success of leading Sergius Paulus to faith in Jesus is the announcement in the very next major place of proclamation, Pisidian Antioch, of his intention to turn toward the Gentiles (Acts 13:46). What is Paul trying to do here? Is he simply seeking to provoke his detractors by announcing that he is turning to the Gentiles and, by implication, away from the Jews? Or is Paul actually shifting his primary focus to the Gentiles?

There are several clues that it is the announcement, rather than an actual change in tactics, that Paul is trying out. Why did Paul have to announce to both the Jews and the Gentiles in attendance that he was turning to the Gentiles and away from the Jews? Why didn't he just go ahead and turn instead of promising—or threatening—to do so? And more importantly, why doesn't the record in Acts indicate that he actually changed his strategy following this announcement? Did he in fact do so? Paul seems to have continued preaching to both Jews and Gentiles in the cities he visits. He tells the Ephesian elders in Melitus at the end of his third journey, for example, that when he had been with them he had "testified to both Jews and Greeks about repentance toward God and faith toward our Lord Jesus" (20:21). Acts ends with Paul welcoming "all who came to him" (28:30).

It cannot be determined from the account in Acts whether Paul had preached to pagan gentile audiences prior to his meeting with Sergius Paulus in Paphos, but what is clear is that he is making a public announcement of turning to the Gentiles after he had already done so, yet he is not actually turning away from the Jewish community. In fact, it is the announcement that assures that Paul will get interested and often hostile audiences within the Jewish communities he visits.

But does the provocative announcement of intentions help achieve Paul's hope that by turning to the Gentiles, and with their acceptance of the gospel, the Jews would be "envious" and accept the gospel as well (Rom 11:11)? Paul must have concluded that this controversial announcement was helpful in gaining the attention of the Jews, for several years later, after resistance from the Jewish community in Corinth, he again proclaims: "From now on I will go to the Gentiles" (Acts 18:6). This is provocative. It ensures that he will be controversial. This guarantees publicity. And even negative publicity helps create an opportunity to preach. This takes us to another high-risk innovation that Paul continues to repeat even after it almost gets him killed.

Public Drama and Confrontation. Luke seems to take care to record the dramatic details of the confrontations between Paul and his many detractors. The details of the almost-lethal resistance by the tenacious group of anti-Paul alarmists who followed Paul and Barnabas from Pisidian Antioch overland to Iconium and Lystra (Acts 14:19), Paul's near death experience of stoning in Lystra followed by his dramatic recovery and bold public return to the city (14:20), and finally his return visits to the very places from which he had just been evicted (14:21), could be evidence that Paul is experimenting with the dangerous drama of public confrontation.

Paul not only provokes the Jewish community in public, he does the same with Roman officials, and in front of non-Jewish crowds. In Philippi, Paul the Roman citizen engages in a dramatic, public provocation of Roman officials. Philippi is another magnificent Roman-style city to which Paul and Silas journey immediately after arriving at the seaport of Neapolis (16:16–40). Here Paul and Silas are attacked by a mob after Paul performs an exorcism on a slave girl who had been making a profit for her owner by telling peoples' fortunes. The slave girls' owners "dragged them into the marketplace before the authorities" (16:19). After listening to the accusations from the mob, the magistrates ordered Paul and Silas to be stripped and beaten in public without a trial. They were then thrown in prison.

All of this was highly irregular and completely illegal treatment of a Roman citizen and begs the question of why Paul did not reveal his citizenship and avoid the pain. More intriguing, however, is the additional deliberate drama that unfolds in the story. On the morning following the midnight earthquake that freed the prisoners who did not escape, and the subsequent conversion of the jailor and his family after Paul prevented him from committing suicide, the magistrates gave orders for Paul and Silas to be released. Had they heard what had happened down at the jail following the earthquake?

"Come out now," they sent word, "go in peace" (16:36).

Now Paul does a little power drama, an act designed to grab the attention of the public in Philippi. He has been silent about his citizenship; now he flaunts it. The time is right to use it to an advantage in order to publicly challenge the very system that gives him the power and privilege he enjoys as a Roman citizen. "They have beaten us in public, uncondemned, men who are Roman citizens, and have thrown us into prison," Paul protests, "and now are they going to discharge us in secret? Certainly not! Let them come and take us out themselves" (16:37).

The Egnatian Way runs right through the center of Philippi and it is on this road where everyone can observe the chagrin of the magistrates as they meekly escort Paul, the Roman citizen they had ordered beaten, out of town. He leaves for Thessalonica, but he has performed an act of the kingdom on his way out of Philippi. Paul, the Roman citizen and follower of Jesus, is experimenting with the public drama of the confrontation between the gospel and the Roman Empire.

This could be called "improvisational theater of the gospel." Paul was learning from and performing for the people who developed and utilized theater to reinforce their conception of the world, their system of good and evil, of power, order, and authority. Paul was performing drama as well, and I cannot help but believe he was thinking ahead as he continued on the Egnatian Way toward Thessalonica, about an encore there.

Paul had experimented with publicly confronting everyone now, fellow followers of Jesus, Jews, Roman officials, and ordinary pagan Gentiles. While personally dangerous, it succeeded in making Paul and the gospel he preached known. It is clear that Paul deemed these impromptu theater performances, this chance to ad-lib the gospel on the public stages of synagogues, theaters, courtrooms, agoras, streets, and even finally in the temple of Jerusalem, as worthy of repeating.

Sailing. Paul is arguably the first Christian missionary to utilize the non-Jewish technology and skills of sailing as a primary means of conveying the good news throughout the Roman Empire. While the relative speed and efficiency of sea travel was obviously integral to the Romanization of the Mediterranean through Rome's military, economic, political, and cultural dominance, it was likely not self-understood that taking the gospel to sea was a good idea. Paul adapted to sea travel to accomplish his mission goals and expanded his ministry as a result of his seafaring.

Seasoned seafarers such as Paul are aware that sailing is more than a mode of transportation. It bears repeating that the sea and seafaring offers an alternative to the land-based ways of understanding the world, oneself, and even life, faith, and God. The awareness of universality is gained in experiencing sea travel and listening to the tales of the sailors of distant places. The extended periods of terror, boredom, and occasional bliss at sea offer time to integrate and reflect. It is very likely that the constant sailing in and out of harbors dominated by monuments of pagan power and the success of the Roman system continued to feed Paul's imagination about the kingdom of God.

Paul's vision of the potential of the gospel developed and expanded as he sailed the pagan sea through the heart of the Roman Empire. He dreamed of ever-longer journeys, even to Spain and beyond, perhaps even to the unexplored regions beyond the storied Gates of Hercules—the Straits of Gibraltar—which the seafarers who surround him doubtlessly discussed during Paul's voyages.

In sailing, Paul was doing more than getting from place to place. He was utilizing pagan, empire-building expertise and technology for the kingdom. He was making connections. Sailing on pagan ships immersed

Paul in its particular sailing traditions, culture, and superstitions, which for the duration of a voyage, take all passengers captive. Paul discovered that seafaring is appropriate for carrying the good news of the kingdom throughout the Roman Empire.

Pagan Philosophy. The rather atypical story in Acts 17 of Paul's time alone in Athens, where he was clearly exploring the religion and culture of this famous city, also includes the account of his attempt to utilize pagan philosophy in introducing and explaining the gospel in its broadest terms. There is no doubt Paul was familiar enough with pagan philosophy to engage the philosophers of Athens on their own terms and, from the story in Acts, actually seemed to do quite well in his speech before his interlocutors on the Areopagus. It is not clear however, whether Paul perceived this to be a success or failure, for although Dionysius the Areopogite accepted the faith, we do not read of Paul attempting to introduce the gospel in quite the same way again. What does seem clear is that Paul is both exploring and experimenting in Athens.

Social Status. Paul's status as a citizen, a highly coveted achievement in the Roman Empire, provided him with high status. However, he did not use his privilege in predictable ways, but seemed to hide his identity as citizen of Rome on some occasions and publicize it on others. Additionally, he even elevated the shame of imprisonment as a symbol and demonstration of his high status as a follower of Jesus. This is an amazing innovation within a status-conscious society, for prison, like crucifixion, was one of the great humiliations within the Roman system. Paul inverted the shame of crucifixion to glory in the example of Jesus. He appropriates his suffering as a way of exposing the flaws of the Roman system of justice and the skewed categories of good and evil, as well as a way of gaining status among the believers.

Gender Relations and Roles. Luke is careful to mention "women of high standing" in Pisidian Antioch (Acts 13:50), Thessalonica, and Berea (17:4, 12) who respond to Paul's preaching. In Philippi it is a woman, Lydia, who is first to be baptized. Then, in a bold move, she insists that Paul, Silas, and Timothy use her home as their base while in Philippi. This they do (16:13–15). In Corinth, Paul has a close working relationship with Priscilla and Aquila, staying in their home, traveling with them to

Ephesus, and working with them in ministry. He names women as his "fellow workers" (Rom 16:3; Phil 4:3).[4]

Pagan Ideals and Role Models. Paul adapts the images of pagan professions, which are foreign or even offensive to Jews, as metaphors and examples for Christians. He draws favorable parallels of the pagan, naked athletes' discipline, commitment, and competitive spirit to that of a follower of Jesus (1 Cor 9:24–26). He holds up the example of the feared and hated Roman soldiers' endurance and total commitment as a model for the "soldier of Christ Jesus" (2 Tim 2:3). Paul, remembering his own feelings of fear in storms at sea and the competence of the pagan sailors, tells the Ephesians not to be "as children, tossed about by the waves, and blown here and there" by enticing false teaching (Eph 4:14).

There are certainly many more examples of Paul's creative innovations seeking to make the gospel relevant, attractive, credible, and effective within the pagan experience of life in the Roman Empire. Not all of Paul's innovations proved to be especially effective. Some of the things Paul did may even have been counterproductive. Is there evidence that he changed tactics based on what did and did not further the cause of sharing the good news? I believe there is. One thing is certain, however: he did not seem to change tactics on the basis of his own well-being or self-preservation.

For Paul, innovation was always a risky enterprise for him personally. Until he tried something once, he could not predict the reaction of his various accusers or listeners. The reactions to Paul's innovations by Jews, Christians, pagans, Roman authorities, and others were never predictable but varied under differing circumstances, times, and places. Crowds especially were unpredictable. Experiments tried in one place did not achieve the same results in another.

Innovation and adaptation was never over for Paul. Paul's creative attempts to connect the gospel to the pagan world through personally risky experimentation with the message of Jesus provide Christians ever since with a universal and timeless model of Christian engagement of culture with the gospel. His theological conclusions about the gospel and its

---

4. Paul had once also been non-discriminatory in his persecution of the early Christians. Luke makes a point of mentioning several times that Paul imprisoned and persecuted both men and women (Acts 8:3, 12; 9:2).

power, application, and attraction in pagan society grew out of his innovation as he explored the Roman Empire. This is a central feature of Paul's example of discipleship. It is the model for faithful living and witness in all other empires.

Paul's Personal Learning

While it is perhaps more important to recognize the contribution Paul made to universalize the gospel message in *how* he learned, it is also fair to examine *what* he learned through his deliberate experiments. Some observations of Paul's general conclusions based on his life as an entrepreneur of the gospel can be made.

Paul writes to the church in Corinth that, "'All things are lawful,' but not all things are not beneficial. 'All things are lawful,' but not all things build up" (1 Cor 10:23). While this passage is generally not applied to his entrepreneurial approach to interpreting and communicating the gospel, it seems appropriate and consistent with the context and Paul's life to apply it in that way. Some principles of the freedom for the believer may be counterproductive to the greater goal of attracting people to the faith. I believe Paul learned that not everything works equally well to demonstrate the validity and attraction of the good news.

Paul has learned of the power of the cross and the hope of the resurrection in his own suffering. He writes,[5] "I have fought a good fight, I have finished the race, I have kept the faith. From now on there is reserved for me the crown of righteousness" (2 Tim 4:7). Here, in this allusion to an athlete's reward, Paul concludes at the end of his life, that every imprisonment, beating, shipwreck, humiliation, and defeat had been worth the personal risk. While his life had been a contradiction of the pagan definitions of success, of goodness, of power and glory, it would be Jesus, the righteous judge, who would be giving the reward. In following Jesus' call in the empire, Paul learned the meaning of life in abundance.

Through experience of both success and failure, Paul learned bold humility, absolute confidence in the power of Jesus in his life, and assurance in the ultimate victory of the gospel in the world of Roman triumph.

5. Or, more likely, someone else writes about Paul based on observations and/or accurate accounts of Paul's testimony at the end of his life.

To the Corinthian Christians Paul wrote, "When I am weak, then I am strong" (2 Cor 12:10). He told the church in Philippi that he could "do all things through him [Christ] who strengthens me" (Phil 4:13).

Paul has learned to know, appreciate, and love the pagans. He writes to the Christians in Rome that "all have sinned and fall short of the glory of God" (Rom 3:23). This statement is not simply a sweeping indictment of human weakness and sin but is also a radical statement of commonality of the human family. Pagans are human, capable of good and evil just as Jews are. All people are created in God's image.

Paul concludes that identity in Jesus erases *all* social divisions, an extraordinary and highly controversial position to take in both the Jewish religious community and the Roman Empire. "There is no longer Jew nor Greek, there is no longer slave nor free, there is no longer male nor female; for all of you are one in Christ Jesus" (Gal 3:28). This is truly a remarkable idea and has immediate results that Paul has not likely anticipated in places like Corinth.[6]

Paul, the ambitious zealot, has learned to be content. "I have learned to be content with whatever I have" (Phil 4:11).

Paul learned far more than is summarized here, far more than he writes about himself. Paul learned to use his curiosity and courage to connect the gospel of Jesus to the lives and imagination of the diverse people of the Roman Empire. Through trial and error he discovered ways of making the good news of the gospel known, credible, relevant, and attractive in the pagan world. Paul had the capacity to learn continuously, adapt his understanding, and adjust his mission approaches to a variety of peoples and contexts. Paul became an effective entrepreneur of the gospel in the Roman Empire. This effectiveness was possible in part because he was a citizen, both of the Roman Empire and of the kingdom of God.

---

6. At least some of Paul's extensive writings that addressed roles of men and women, slaves and masters, poor and wealthy can be seen as the necessary transitional guidelines dealing with the unanticipated results of the dismantling of some of the rigid social divisions. It is difficult to incorporate sudden social change into groups of people who have much to gain or lose by those changes. The letter to the Corinthians makes this clear.

The Church Is like a Ship at Sea

If, as Rodney Stark asserts, the vast majority of the churches in the Roman Empire at the end of the first century were in port cities,[7] it is no surprise that the church was depicted as a ship in some of the early Christian art. Although neither Paul nor these seaport Christians were afraid to travel on the sea, they also were aware that they could not control its capricious nature. On the other hand, by utilizing the uncontrolled power of wind and waves, the sailors could guide the ship forward, taking the people on it toward their destination.

On a first-century ship you could not chose your fellow travelers. It is doubtful that Paul could have eaten kosher or observe the Sabbath very well on a sea voyage with a motley crew of pagans and Jews, slaves and free, men and women, an experience that likely shaped his understanding of the church. First-century cargo ships were floating collections of human diversity, united by a common destination and cooperating to reach it alive. What a picture of the church! This reliance on others' skills and experience was absolutely critical aboard a first-century ship, or church, whether these sailors were Jewish or pagan, slave or free, rich or poor, male or female.

The church, like the first-century ships carrying wheat from Alexandria to Rome, took constant risks, sometimes with disaster, as the shipwreck story in Acts 27 attests. But the rewards made the risks worth taking for both first-century grain ships and the first-century church.

We now look at those risks and rewards. For living by faith in the twenty-first century, as in the first, is like sailing.

7. Stark, *Cities of God*, 76.

part 3

Living by Faith Is Like Sailing

I WELL REMEMBER THE borderline terror I experienced when, after having lived securely aboard *SailingActs* in the Volos harbor and outfitting her for the voyage ahead, my wife and I finally started the motor and untied the stiff ropes of our untested boat. Planning, preparation, commitments, investment, sweat, and tears, all of these were part of the experience up until that point, but the sheer adrenalin-fueled combination of dread and excitement as we cast off made everything during the pre-launch phase seem almost pleasant and mundane in comparison.

In the first month of injuries, storms, bungled berthing, equipment failure, and unexpected delays from belligerent officials hoping for a little cash, we learned to sail. We also learned to trust the boat, ourselves, each other, absolute strangers, and God. Sailing unfamiliar seas toward unknown destinations is like following Jesus into the world, like living by faith in changing times and uncertain future. It is living a kind of life in abundance, with far more trials and tribulations and far more rewards and blessings, far more of everything it seems, just as Jesus promised.

Paul was used to sailing. Successful navigation in the first-century Mediterranean was done by men who had learned through trial and error, who remembered the hazards and how to avoid them even in the dark, who anticipated the storms and how to survive them when all hope seemed lost. There were no instruments or charts and very few navigational aids.

Paul, the sailor of the Mediterranean, can be seen as a first-century navigator for Christians living in the great port cities of the Mediterranean. The early Christian movement in the Roman Empire was like a ship sailing the sea, for progress and survival depended on capable navigation through the uncertain times and uncharted waters.

6

The Christian Movement
in the Mediterranean

The Voyage toward the Kingdom in the Roman Empire

RECENTLY I MADE A four-day voyage on *SailingActs* from Ashkelon, Israel to Finike on the southern coast of Turkey. Two former students were aboard as crew. One of the students had some sailing experience, the other had none. As we made the final preparations, boarded, untied the dock lines, motored out of the marina entrance, and pointed the bow toward Turkey, I experienced the familiar flood of emotions—the combined anticipation and trepidation unique to embarking on a passage over open waters. I have never noticed these feelings at such high levels when boarding an airplane or setting out on a road trip. The difference has nothing to do with the destination.

It is the sea that makes the difference, for while the wind's power and effects is completely beyond human control, we must cooperate and utilize that power to make any progress when sailing. No wind, no progress. Too much wind, great peril. Unfavorable wind, indirect route. So when you set out to sea, you never know what to expect, how long the voyage will take or, in fact, whether you will actually make it at all. Sea voyages are always journeys of deliberate risk, of competing and cooperating with the unpredictable and uncontrollable wind and waves. One sails by faith.

But this is not foolhardy risk, or naïve faith. This kind of faith is based on realistic confidence in a well-maintained boat, committed and trustworthy crew, accurate charts and cruising guides, reliable instruments, and plenty of extra supplies of food and water. It is a faith grounded on the advice and encouragement of others who have made similar voyages. It is a faith in one's own abilities, earned through experience of overcoming challenges on previous voyages.

As we were leaving the safety of the marina in Ashkelon, Reuben, the Israeli sailing instructor who keeps his boat in the marina, and who sees everyone he meets as in urgent need of his advice, gave his usual unsolicited counsel. "Remember, if the wind is not on your nose," he said, "you have made a mistake in your navigation. You are not in the Mediterranean." We laughed but we knew Rueben was only partly joking. For it seems that regardless of which direction you attempt to sail in the Mediterranean, most of the time that is precisely the direction from which the wind is blowing.

In the first century, this most likely also seemed to be the case for those aboard the early church-ship in the empire. Paul's letters to the Christians living in the great Mediterranean seaports can be viewed as guidelines for navigating the powerful, unstable, unpredictable, pagan sea of the Roman Empire. Aboard ships and waiting in port cities around the Mediterranean, Paul had time to observe, conceive ideas, and contemplate advice that he would put in his letters. These letters addressed the hazards of the sea-like world of the Roman Empire and the potential of the kingdom for those who had joined the voyage toward it.

Immersed in the pagan world, surrounded by the displays of its success, reminded of its power to reward and punish, relating daily to people who believed its enticing promises, Paul succeeded in making the power of the crucified Jesus of Nazareth and promises of the kingdom credible and attractive to the pagan inhabitants of the Roman Empire.[1] In cities, especially the port cities of the Mediterranean, people actually believed Paul

---

1. The themes of "power" and "the powers" in Paul's theology has been the subject of a vast amount of extremely important theological work. Some key contributions have been made by Arnold, *Powers of Darkness*; Berkhof, *Christ and the Powers*; Wink, *Naming the Powers*; and Yoder, *Politics of Jesus*.

and his message and a fledgling movement began to grow. How could this movement that contradicted the patterns of empire be sustained?

The Christian movement and Paul's amazingly effective alternative message of the good news of Jesus and the coming kingdom must be examined within the framework of a system of control that was succeeding to order the Mediterranean world. We will examine some of the characteristics of the success of the Roman Empire in relationship to the dynamic cross-movement of the kingdom within it by looking at the diagram below.

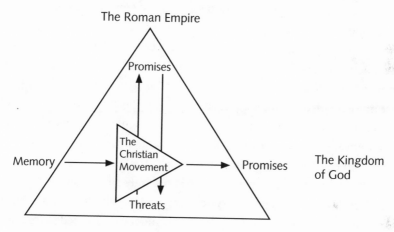

FIGURE 6.1. The Christian Movement in the Roman Empire

While the shape of the Roman Empire is the picture of stability, this is an illusion. Those who have faith in the promises of empire believe that its stability is real; its promises are reliable now and will continue to be so in the future. But as Paul writes to the Corinthians living in that most impressive, powerful, wealthy seaport, "what can be seen is temporary, but what cannot be seen is eternal" (2 Cor 4:18b). From Paul's creation-based perspective of empire and his encounter with Jesus, it is the kingdom that is eternal and will ultimately succeed. The empire is temporary and will finally vanish, contrary to the promises of those in power and the faith of those who believe those promises and serve the empire.

A visit today to the archeological site of ancient Corinth makes Paul's observations to the Corinthians abundantly clear. Indeed, on the remains of the *bema* on which Paul's hearing before the proconsul, Gallio, was conducted following an accusation of treason against Paul (Acts 18:12–17), the quote from Paul in 2 Cor 4:18, cited above, is inscribed. As one stands on that same *bema* in the heart of a once bustling city of abundance, the once-exquisite columns and capitals lying in the dust give silent affirmation to Paul's observation.

Let's recall that empire is an *attempt* by humans who, separated from the life-sustaining Creator, seek to create the conditions of stability for life by controlling all contingencies and eliminating anything or anyone that threatens it. This kind of stability is always temporary, and comes at great cost, especially to the majority of people in the empire who provide the broad and solid foundation of the system in which they toil.

At the very bottom of the structure were the lowest of the slaves and poor laborers who worked in the mines and other dangerous and unbearable industries. At the very top of the structure were the ruling elite, the extended families of incredibly wealthy landowners, members of the senate, and other privileged and powerful men. Enormous effort and expense were invested by those at the top who enjoyed the vast wealth, status, and control, to keep the system intact. The tiny minority at the top was ready at any time and place to crush, not only all attempts by anyone to undermine or destabilize the system, but anyone who might potentially do so, including those in the Christian movement who seemed to threaten the status quo of the privileged.

The diagram above depicts the fundamental contrasts of the Christian movement to the structure of the Roman Empire. It is the Christian movement that is obviously unstable and vulnerable, and indeed, is inherently so. But stability and security are not the goal. The voyage toward the kingdom is perilous and unstable because it is in an empire that views it as disruptive and that will eventually seek to control the movement by utilizing the empire's arsenal of both good and evil.

In contrast to the static and stable shape of the empire, the sustainability of the Christian movement is dependent on its orientation and momentum toward the promises of the kingdom. Its vision of goodness, justice, healing, and eternal life is oriented not toward the top of what is, but in the direction of what will be, as promised by Jesus and explained by Paul. This orientation is what keeps the movement going. While the biblical study maps demonstrate the general feature of biblical faith as a literal movement out of or through empires, Acts and its study maps tell a story that includes social and cultural movement within the Roman Empire as well.

The movement's momentum toward the promises is fueled by hope in the future. The future, rather than the past, determines the direction and shape of the movement in the present. When "everything has become new" (2 Cor 5:17) there is no tradition, no history, no ingrained social patterns that can be used as criteria adequate for setting the trajectory. It is the future promises that shape, not only the present, but the way history is interpreted. While memory is important for orienting the movement toward the future, the promises of the future change the memories of the past, or at least the meaning of those memories.

This alternative society can only exist when there is momentum and power operative within it. The moment the forward movement toward the kingdom ceases, the future-oriented horizontal pyramid will become an upward-oriented vertical pyramid. It will "conform to the world" and become aligned with society's patterns of good and evil. It may continue to exist in this position, but it will no longer be a Christian movement. It will be another voluntary society patterned after other voluntary associations of the empire.[2]

In stark contrast to the empire, in the Christian movement there are no fixed patterns of authority, no rewards and punishments meted out by the leaders. Everyone, potentially at least, is a full participant, and instability, even chaos and constant adjustment, is a feature of the movement.[3] Authority is not exercised within the vertical good/evil patterns of the empire but rather the horizontal toward/away differences in the kingdom in relation to Jesus' promises and invitation to follow. Authority is not exercised from the top but from the front. Authority is earned through leadership toward the vision by persons who embody the vision in their life, who represent Jesus most clearly, who demonstrate Jesus' power, and

2. "In the cosmopolitan and mobile Mediterranean world . . . voluntary associations were a widespread phenomenon in urban settings. . . . They . . . permitted a sense of social mobility within a society whose class distinctions were otherwise ridged and impermeable" (Crossan and Reed, *In Search*, 47).

3. There are numerous clear examples of the instability of the Christian movement recorded in Acts, and the ongoing creative attempts to establish order in the chaos. The selection of the seven deacons in response to the discrimination of the Hellenistic Jewish widows in Acts 6 is one good example.

who share in his suffering. Authority is shared by those who exercise it and who enable others to move toward leadership positions in the front as they mature and use their gifts in ways that contribute to the progress of the movement as a whole.

The final feature depicted on the diagram is the position of the movement of the kingdom within the empire. It is not at the top nor does it seek to be. It is in the position of the Old Testament prophets, in the lower middle of the pyramid. It lives and grows in the similar social location as that of its leader, Jesus, and of its emissary, Paul. As long as the Christian movement identifies itself with and relates to those who "hunger and thirst for righteousness," as long as it relates to the empire as Jesus and Paul did, the movement will never find itself at the top of the social pyramid, nor will it resemble those who are there.

But neither is the movement at the bottom of the pyramid. Part of the attraction of the kingdom for those at the bottom is for immediate change to their life. The immediate life-changing physical and social benefits of joining the movement are evident in the very first chapters of Acts, and are verified in the attraction of the lower classes to the movement. The Christian movement is in the position to attract those from both extremes of the pyramid, and to bring them together into a radically different social entity than that of the empire.

Perils of the Voyage

Because the movement cuts across the patterns of positive and negative control that give stability to the empire, it is a voyage marked by turbulence. The power to punish those who threaten the status quo of the system of control on one hand, and power to reward those who reinforce it on the other, is firmly in the hands of those at the top of the pyramid. Those at the top have virtually unlimited ability to violently coerce, punish, and eliminate the troublemakers.

There are also vast resources to promise rewards and deliver on those promises—a share in the power and the glory that they, the tiny group of the elite on top, enjoy. As long as most of the inhabitants of the empire between the top and the bottom of the pyramid are oriented toward the top, the order of the system is secure and ensures stability of the pyramid.

This power of good and evil exercised by the elite is a hazard on which the church-ship can founder or be diverted away from the course toward the promises of the kingdom. We will look at both evil and its threats, and the good and its promises, and the effects that acquiescence in the face of either had on the Christian movement.

Examples of violent suppression of movements of faith by empires abound in history and in the biblical story. The New Testament opens with the nativity story that includes Herod's slaughtering of all male infants under age two after hearing that a "king" had been born in Bethlehem (Matt 2:16–17). Extreme measures such as these were not only carried out as a kind of preemptive strike against future threats, real or imagined, they were designed to demonstrate the consequences of rebellion to the populace who might have been tempted to rebel. Terror was a common weapon of both the rulers and the ruled in ancient empires, but only the rulers had the legitimate right to use terror in their attempt to keep the empire stable.

The patron/client relationship, a feature within the Roman Empire,[4] was both stable and static, fixing patterns of patronage and dependency for generations. To be in a client relationship with a powerful and wealthy patron was one of the ways of sharing some of the power and social status while contributing to that of the patron's.

Status change, while not impossible, was extremely difficult. While the obvious benefits of higher status motivated many to spend their lives submissively, diligently carrying out their responsibilities in the hopes of achieving some wealth, freedom, citizenship, or other forms of social status, actual change of status was seldom sudden or of great significance. What were the choices of the non-elite in the Roman Empire? Soldiers serving their twenty-five years of deprivation and danger, slaves faithfully serving mediocre or low-status masters for most of their lives, gladiators surviving lethal contests, all had their eyes fixed on the promise of reward—freedom, wealth, a plot of land, and most of all citizenship, which would give them status in the system and a chance to display it in front of those who had not achieved as much.

---

4. For a thorough description of social class and status in the Roman Empire, see Jeffers, *Greco-Roman World*, 180–96. The question of how Paul's father or grandfather had obtained citizenship is a widely debated issue.

So while the power and glory flaunted by the privileged elite from the very top of the pyramid was painfully visible to the many on the lower ranks below, it was not enjoyed by most of them. The promises were at best only partially fulfilled for the poor majority. Their experiences did not match their expectations. Disillusionment and simmering resentment lurked below the surface throughout the broad base of the empire, making the maintenance of the system a continuous and difficult process.

Rome's expansion of the empire did not change the shape of the pyramid, only its size. The ruling elite recognized that any expansion of the size of the privileged group on the very peak of the pyramid would necessitate a proportional expansion of the base of the pyramid if they were to retain the level of power and glory they were enjoying, and the wealth necessary to maintain their position.

An explanatory system, a view of reality, a religion, or a philosophy that persuades, manipulates, and directs the hearts and the minds of people so that their compliance within the social order is voluntary is the most effective way of maintaining the system of privilege and status within any empire. When everyone from slaves to rulers are convinced that the way things are is the way they should be, or is the way the gods intended, or is the best hope for humanity and them personally, then very little coercion is needed to keep things under control. Only a persuasive, charismatic leader with a counter-message and little to lose might pose a threat. In this case swift and sever punishment would be necessary, preferably before the charismatic individual could convince the masses of another view of reality, another religious possibility, another set of promises that contradicts the officially approved versions. Status differentiation that greatly benefits the few and deprives the many of those benefits necessitates constant religious, cultural, and philosophical reinforcement, constant vigilance, and occasionally massive coercive measures.

Official ideology that explains the nature of the world, that controls the definitions of good and evil, that justifies the way things are or explains how they should be, is a powerful tool in the hands of the elite at the top. While official ideology in an empire may not appear to be oppressive, it always favors the status quo, legitimizes state violence, and the repression of others. Domination, brutality, and injustice can all be justified as good. Absolute power did not only corrupt absolutely in the Roman Empire, it gave the elite the characteristics of their gods and demonstrated the gods' blessing. In the Roman Empire, as in other ancient empires, absolute power made one absolutely divine. The divine emperor relied on the national "priests" to ensure acquiescence and to maintain control of the system.

These respected authorities publicized and popularized the official ideological and religious framework of the empire. Their function was to explain reality, focus hopes, promote the promises, laud the good, identify and ridicule the evil, define the enemy, and orient the hearts and the minds of the people toward compliance and cooperation. These were the empire's "official intellectuals" at the service of the ruling elite to convince the masses of the rightness of their own lower status, as well as the legitimate avenues for improvement of their lives.

Poets and playwrights immortalized and popularized the myths, the heroes, and the gods that shaped and maintained the worldview of the populace. Priests officiating at important public and private moments of celebration and transition reinforced the awareness of divine order for the inhabitants of the empire. Philosophers interpreted the world, defined goodness and evil, and promoted corresponding moral behavior for the people. Politicians explained their actions in terms the official myths, the emperor embodied them, and the empire's historians interpreted the present in terms of them.

The overwhelming presence of pagan myths, ideals, dreams, and promises was everywhere. Monuments of the success of paganism and human achievement stood in every harbor, on the roads from the harbor to the city, on every high place in the cities. In the theaters and the *agoras*, in the *stoas* and the stadiums, in the temples and the palaces, in the public baths and even in the public latrines, the power and glory of the gods and the achievements of their human representatives were flaunted and celebrated in every aspect of life.

Those brave individuals who, like the prophets of the Hebrew Scriptures, had challenged the religious speculations of the priests, the abuses of power of the rulers, the hypocrisy of the philosophers, or false assumptions of the poets and playwrights, were generally tolerated only as long as their message had little influence. If their message diverged too far from that of the official intellectuals, and especially if this began to be too popular among the masses, or if it seemed that a breakdown of civil order was immanent because of their influence, they were executed.[5]

Yet in spite of the continuous reinforcement of the divine and political myths, in spite of the brutal elimination of alternative voices, the problem of death still haunted the lives of everyone in the empire regardless of status. Then as now, in spite of the relentless quest to maximize and prolong life, death was also always close at hand. People died at home. Accidental and malicious death occurred in urban areas. Crucifixion was done in public. Death, in the Roman Empire, was even a spectator sport.

Gladiatorial combat was a way of dealing with the problem of death in an empire that promised abundance in life but could not give life itself. Often viewed today as merely bloodthirsty entertainment of the violent, debauched masses desperate for diversion, more recent interpretations into the culture of gladiatorial combat have challenged the popular views of this bloody spectacle. Gladiatorial contests were elaborate, all-day events, costing fortunes, and were often sponsored by members of the wealthy ruling class as a way of boosting their popularity with the lower classes.

According to the evidence this was far more than entertainment. These spectacles allowed the people of the empire to confront death and chaos personally and to vicariously overcome these life-threatening evils through the victory of the gladiators. The execution of criminals reassured people that the evil in their midst was being addressed and held at bay. The gladiator fights allowed people to participate in the triumph of life over death, for the spectators had the power to determine the fate of the gladiators. Worthy fighters could be allowed to live, and eventually be given their freedom. They could also be summarily executed if deemed unworthy, without any more process than the voice of the crowd.[6]

---

5. Socrates is one of the more famous examples whose popular intellectual power threatened the stability and order of Athenian society, provoking the rulers to sentence him to death. Even pagan prophets could pose a threat to the pagan rulers.

6. This interpretation comes from a special display on gladiatorial combat in Ephesus at the Ephesus Museum in Selçuk, Turkey. Does the death penalty in America perhaps serve the same function? Or how about the entertainment industry with its fixation on bloody violence and the triumph of good over evil? Is not this a contemporary example of the "value" of the gladiator contests that allows spectators to triumph over death at least momentarily?

The victory parades, in which the defeated prisoners of war were marched through the streets in chains and either executed or enslaved, was a triumph over the threat of death for all of the inhabitants of the empire as well. Death itself was being paraded in defeat, and the celebration at the defeat or death of the enemy was a celebration of life. Death, it seemed, was being defeated and destroyed. This theme of living through the death of the evil other was repeated endlessly in entertainment in the Roman Empire. This is still a major form of entertainment in contemporary society.

Competing Promises of Empire and Kingdom

The direction and the position of the Christian movement, cutting across the vertical patterns of the empire, is one of great risk. The fundamental difference of orientation and direction guarantees both connections with, and disturbance of, the established social and religious patterns of the world. This is the position of Jesus that made his death on the cross inevitable. The movement of his followers, if it is authentically on the way of Jesus, will be similar. This is the "cross-movement" of Jesus that cuts across the social patterns of empire.

The cross-movement toward the kingdom ensures that the participants of the movement encounter the constant enticements and threats of the empire. While each person who joins the movement remains in the empire, his or her value to the empire is greatly diminished for it will no longer be possible to promise or threaten that person to serve the interests of the empire unreservedly. The movement is vulnerable for it does not utilize evil to protect itself.

As in the empire, the movement of the kingdom is shaped by the explanatory myths that offer interpretations of the world as experienced, that present meaning for life and give hope for its improvement, that make promises about the future, and that describe rewards both in the present and beyond death. As in the empire, persons with authority also interpret and explain the reality of present life and the responsibilities, privileges, and responsibilities of the kingdom movement. These interpretations however, stand in diametric opposition to that of the official intellectuals of the empire listed above. Why would anyone have believed these alternative explanations of reality? Paul faced this challenge repeatedly.

A brief excursion into a Marxist theory of the power of ideas may help to appreciate the kind of power and authority operative in the movement of the kingdom so clearly demonstrated by Paul within the Roman Empire.

The role of religion in history as a tool of oppression by the ruling classes, the "opiate of the people" that helps the lower classes accept their suffering and pain as producers, has been accurately described and critiqued by Karl Marx. In Marx's vision, the process of emancipation from the oppression of the wealthy, powerful, elite class would begin as the workers became aware of the lies by which they were being manipulated, controlled, and exploited, and would be realized eventually through violent revolution. Marxist philosophers were the new prophets, exposing workers to the "truth" that would set them free. Marx, no stranger to the Hebrew Scriptures, recognized the patterns of religiously sanctioned slavery of ancient and modern empires as well as the themes of liberation from slavery in the story of the exodus from Egypt.

Antonio Gramsci, another Marxist philosopher who once led the Italian communist party and eventually died as a political prisoner under Mussolini in 1937, developed an alternative interpretation. According to Gramsci, the historical role of intellectuals belonging to the ruling elite was to keep the masses content with their own bondage. He called these intellectuals "traditional intellectuals." In addition, throughout history, other kinds of intellectuals—"organic intellectuals" in Gramsci's terminology—have challenged the traditional intellectuals. These are the charismatic leaders and popular prophets from among the lower classes. Gramsci recognized with appreciation the power of organic intellectuals in challenging the official sanctioned oppression of empire. In contrast to Marx, Gramsci noted that popular religious movements in history were often also social movements of political liberation.[7]

Organic intellectuals, including religious leaders, according to Gramsci, exercise power by connecting an alternative vision of the future to the experienced life of the poor and the powerless. These organic intellectuals may originate from among the elite and may, through their

---

7. For an extensive treatment of Gramsci's theory of the exercise of power by "traditional intellectuals" to support the status quo, and "organic intellectuals" to change it, see pp. 23–68 of my doctoral dissertation, "Gramsci's Theory."

education or other achievements, begin their careers as traditional intellectuals. But in contrast to the traditional intellectuals who support and benefit from the status quo, organic intellectuals may voluntarily identify with the disenfranchised in their opposition to the elite. They speak their language, offer hope of a better future, and suffer with them. Their power is in their ability to demonstrate the validity of their claims in their own person, to make their claims credible and immediate for all. When you look at the organic intellectual, according to Gramsci, the reality of their promises are visible. They embody their message.

The usefulness of Gramsci's penetrating analysis for understanding the power and appeal of biblical characters such as Moses, Isaiah, Amos, Jesus, and Paul, or such diverse modern prophets such as Mahatma Gandhi, Dr. Martin Luther King Jr., and Nelson Mandela, is obvious. What is especially helpful is Gramsci's recognition of the attraction to the disenfranchised, disappointed, and disillusioned of joining a positive, promising movement toward emancipation, even if there is high risk involved. For those who have experienced *meaningless* suffering and involuntary deprivation in life, *meaningful* suffering is infinitely more fulfilling and rewarding. With little to lose and much to gain by believing the attractive promises for immediate and long-term change for which they desperately long, the risk of suffering and even death at the hands of the authorities is worth it. This pattern is can be observed wherever revolution occurs.

For Gramsci, those whose hearts and minds have been persuaded by the validity of the new explanations of life and whose life has meaning and purpose within that new framework, whose experiences of deprivation and suffering make sense and have value, those people comprise a voluntary, powerful new movement. This powerful movement may pose a threat for the ruling elite, for participants in this kind of alternative social movement can no longer be manipulated by either rewards or threats of violence and death from the rulers. Thus whenever voluntary, popular social movements that are fundamentally at odds with the systems of empires begin, they inevitably engender brutal and violent reaction from the ruling classes. This effort is usually, but not always, successful.

Paul communicated and demonstrated the good news of Jesus and the kingdom in powerfully relevant ways that connected with the hopes and aspirations, as well as the experience of life, of the disenfranchised, disappointed, and disillusioned majority of the empire. Paul's message focused on the power of Jesus, which contrasted so clearly with the power exercised and exhibited by the Roman Empire. Jesus' power was relevant in how it contradicted the power of the empire and was available for the pagan believer to appropriate immediately in life.

For Paul, Jesus' power is demonstrated on the cross, the Roman instrument of torture, intimidation, and death. By not avoiding the cross, Jesus triumphed in two ways. One, Jesus was not intimidated by the threat of the cross on his life, and two, he triumphed over the finality and effectiveness of the cross and death itself in his resurrection. The power of the cross in the kingdom is the powerlessness of the cross in the empire. If crucifixion isn't effective, what is?! This defeat of the fear of death holds incredible attraction to those in the empire who fear death in all its forms, but especially a cruel death at the hand of the empire.

The power of Jesus displayed on the cross and in the resurrection demonstrated for Paul God's triumph over evil and the ability to deliver those who believe from the slavery and death of any and all evil and systems of evil, human and spiritual.[8] The gospel, Paul declares, "is the power of God for salvation to everyone who has faith" (Rom 1:16). The immediate and ultimate power of the cross is the power over sin and its consequences, death. Everyone is the slave of sin, but through the power of the cross forgiveness and victory over that power can be experienced. How this contrasts to the message of Dionysus, who embodied the attractive "good" of lust that overpowers human resistance! How freeing the message of the power of the gospel to break the slavery of sin must have sounded to the disillusioned of the empire who had tried the promises of Dionysus and a host of other gods and found them to be empty, unfulfilling, and enslaving!

Paul communicated the power of Jesus and the promises of the kingdom in his person. He publicly performed the power of weakness and the glory of shame before the watching audiences. He performed the kingdom on the empire's stages. How did Paul shape the movement toward effectiveness and sustainability?

8. God's power in Jesus is available for the believer against the tyranny of the "principalities and powers." Paul's use of this seems to indicate the rebellious, systemic cooperation of humans with the evil spirits of rebellion normally hidden from human detection, but exposed in Scripture.

We return to the concept of Paul's "experimental theater" to examine several additional key features of Paul's powerful demonstrative and explanatory announcement of the good news of the kingdom in the public arenas of the empire. Experimental theater refers to Paul's dramatic confrontation, demonstration, celebration, proclamation, and explanation of the good news of Jesus. Paul's enactment of the gospel could be seen as theater because his script is the drama of Jesus that Paul was convinced needed to be presented over and over in all times and places. Paul himself had glimpsed the power and triumph of the living Lord. Paul recognized that Jesus' representatives must make Jesus' power and triumph visible to all humanity. Paul's theater of the gospel was experimental, for the stage was now the ends of the earth rather than Palestine, and the freedom and necessity to ad lib the script, in new, provocative, winsome, and relevant ways was necessary.

Paul engaged in "dramatic confrontation" with Jewish detractors, Greek businesspersons, and Roman officials. The pattern of confrontation as a means of demonstrating the power of the gospel and exposing the hypocrisy of the good inhabitants of the empire, both Jew and pagan, began at Paphos, Cyprus at the beginning of the first missionary journey, and continued through his life, when it ended at the temple in Jerusalem at the end of his third mission journey. The final chapters of Acts tell the story of Paul confronting the Roman Empire as a result of his final dramatic confrontation in Jerusalem.

Another feature of Paul's performance of the good news of the kingdom could be called "dramatic demonstration." This display of the power of the gospel was in Paul's personal experiences of suffering and hardship, ranging from public stoning, beatings, imprisonments, shipwreck, poverty, hunger, and cold. The list, which Paul himself compiles, goes on and on. Not only does Paul endure such things, he boasts in them, publicizes them, shows how, in spite of all he has endured, he has not been intimidated into silence. On the contrary, he boasts about these adversities and dangers. Paul is demonstrating, not just the hardships, but the power of Jesus that enables him to continue. He is reenacting the life of Jesus on the public stage of the empire.[9]

9. See 2 Cor 11:25 for the complete list of incredible hardships and experiences about which Paul writes.

Another feature of Paul's performance of the good news of the kingdom in the empire was the reenactment of the good news in "dramatic celebration." When the Jewish and pagan believers met together at the end of Sabbath on the first day of the week,[10] they were publicly celebrating the life of the risen Lord in their joyous worship. The instructions for speaking in tongues, among other things, indicate that worship often had spectators present. The celebration of the Lord's Supper is the dramatic celebration of life over death, an alternative to the gladiator spectacles. The same is true of the public rituals of baptism, and the annual celebrations of Jesus' resurrection later. When we realize the confrontational and threatening nature that the celebration of Jesus' death and resurrection must have posed for the Roman authorities and their official intellectuals who maintained the pagan myths of the empire, we can appreciate the power of dramatic celebration.

Paul was a master of "dramatic proclamation" performed on some of the most awesome stages of the empire—on the Areopagus in Athens in the shadow of the Parthenon, in the palace of Felix and Festus in the magnificent city of Caesarea, on the steps of the Antonio Fortress on the temple mount in Jerusalem, and, although not recorded, perhaps before Nero in Rome itself. Paul's powerful speeches were acts of sheer drama, performed in the very places where the politicians, philosophers, and military generals gave their stirring, empire-building speeches. The spectators would not have missed the point of Paul's message, for his words were only part of the message. The pagan monumental backdrops, the impassioned audiences, and the confused Roman authorities were all part of the drama.

Finally Paul, in a kind of one-man show, utilized "dramatic explanation" to demonstrate the alternative definitions of power and triumph in the kingdom that Jesus had embodied. His suffering at the hands of Jews, Romans, and plain criminals; his shame of imprisonment; his public

10. The "first day of the week" in the Book of Acts, written within the framework of the Jewish measurement of days, began around sundown on Sabbath. Meeting "on the first day of the week" at the end of the Jewish Sabbath enabled the Christians, both Jewish and pagan, from all walks of life to meet together. This would have been very difficult on Sunday morning due to the work obligations of Jews, pagans, and slaves. The story of Eutychus falling asleep during Paul's sermon in Troas makes this clear. "On the first day of the week we met to break bread. Paul was holding a discussion with them; since he intended to leave the next day, he continued speaking until midnight" (Acts 20:7).

humiliation by flogging; his endurance of ill health, travel hardships, lone-liness, and abandonment; his weakness; his manual labor; his struggle with the flesh, are not only revealed by Paul himself, but used as a way of demonstrating the power and triumph of the life of the living Jesus in his own life.

While this use of public humiliation, shame, low status, and weak-ness is incredibly unique in the empire to demonstrate anything positive, it is completely consistent with the example of Jesus, and as such it has tremendous impact, especially among those who have low status them-selves. In the kingdom, their own suffering and low status have value. Paul makes the good news attractive, even the suffering part, for he acts out the meaning of Jesus' words, "Blessed are the poor, for theirs is the kingdom."

We can now summarize Paul's dramatic one-person act of the gospel. Like Jesus, Paul embodied the promises of the kingdom and the inevi-tability of the cross. His authority was not from the top, but was earned through the consistency of his life with his message. Paul's authority was recognized in his close identity with Jesus, especially in his suffering. Paul's ability to demonstrate the realistic promises of the good news made his message powerful and concrete.

Paul's ability to connect the good news of the gospel to the life ex-perience of the diverse pagan inhabitants of the empire, and to identify with the excluded, the deprived, the disappointed, and the disillusioned at all levels, enabled him to make the good news immediate, accessible, and attractive. Paul the leader was a follower of Jesus, the one who leads his people toward the promise from the front, not the top. Like Jesus, Paul had the option of utilizing the power of the world and his status as a citizen of the empire to seek to establish the kingdom of God. But he had already tried that before and, after catching a glimpse of the living Jesus in the presence of the glory of God, he chose to identify with Jesus and his example in a life of suffering for others as he proclaimed the triumph of the kingdom. When Paul did exercise his rights as a citizen within the empire, it was not for his personal benefit or to avoid suffering, but for the sake of the gospel and those who joined the movement of the kingdom.

For Paul, Jesus was not only the author of the script. Jesus was the director of the drama, the manager of the stage, and the only valid critic of his performance of the good news of the kingdom in the public stage of the empire.

The Effects of the Movement of the Kingdom in the Empire

One final feature of the power and promise of Jesus in the movement of the kingdom within the power and glory of the Roman Empire needs to be examined—the effects of the movement on the empire itself. While the participants in the movement of the kingdom in the Roman Empire experienced some of the promises of Jesus only partially, their empire-shaped patterns of life and their relationship to the authorities of the empire, began to change immediately. Liberated from both the enticement of rewards and the threats of punishment from those above on the social pyramid, the movement was impossible to control by the normally effective tools of persuasion and enticement, or intimidation and coercion. It became increasingly difficult for the Roman authorities to ignore the movement due to its popularity and growth.

Like public entertainment, the drama of the kingdom movement was played out in the public of the empire. Like gladiatorial combat, the themes of life and death, victory and defeat, were visibly demonstrated, but this time in direct competition with the life and death of the empire. Was not public martyrdom, sometimes performed in the very same arenas as the gladiatorial spectacles, an attempt to reinforce Rome's triumph over the Christian movement? Were not the faith, defiance, and honor of those martyrs visible to the spectators who, as gladiatorial experts, recognized honor when they saw it? Imagine the consternation of the sponsors of entertainment by martyrdom, as large portions of the crowds were favorably impressed by the Christian martyrs. The movement of the kingdom in the empire not only displayed the weakness of the cross to threaten the Christians, but the power of the cross to expose the weakness of the empire, which could no longer threaten people into submission.

The pressure for the movement to conform to the enticements and the threats of the empire was relentless. The threat of deprivation of the good and the experience of evil was ongoing. In spite of this unrelenting pressure, the stubborn non-conformity of the movement of the kingdom as it gained adherents began to change the patterns of good and evil and the assumptions about power and glory of the pagan system necessary for the success of the Roman Empire.

Life is lonely for those at the top if those below you are no longer envious, no longer desiring to achieve that which you represent, and are living lives oriented in a fundamentally different direction. Like contemporary celebrities, being ignored and forgotten is a far worse fate than notoriety. If neither the promises nor the threats are effective, the power of the elite to control everyone else for their own benefit dissipates.

Was the growing concern of the Roman rulers in the face of the growing movement of the kingdom a reasonable one? Did the promise of eternal life based on the hope in the resurrection of Jesus actually overcome the fear of death in Jesus' followers, making Rome's death threats irrelevant and powerless? This was surely the case for Jesus. This was clearly the claim that Paul made and exemplified in his life and in his own eventual death in Rome. In any case, the movement continued to grow.

Something had to change. The empire's patterns of good and evil begin to shift. Some official intellectuals begin to redefine the good of the empire, imbuing them with new values. Out of self-interest, as the evil exercised from the top becomes increasingly brutal and less effective, popular support for persecution against Christians declines. Society begins to incorporate, albeit slowly and inconsistently, some of the obviously beneficial and positive values of the kingdom demonstrated in the life within the movement. The elite allow it to happen, for they really cannot do otherwise forever. Jesus alluded to this phenomenon in his parables of the kingdom of God. We add these changes to the diagram below.

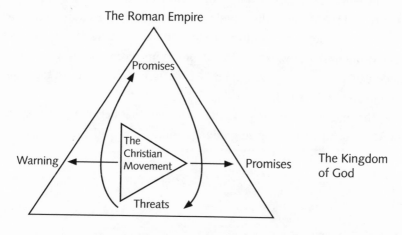

FIGURE 6.2. The Failure of Evil in the Roman Empire

But this is not where history of either the Roman Empire or the Christian movement ends. Perhaps the most seductive temptation of all faced by the movement of the kingdom in the empire was when the elite at the top of the pyramid, in failing to eliminate the movement or intimidate it into alignment with the patterns of the empire, sought to accommodate the movement.

While Rome was failing, the Christian movement was succeeding. By the beginning of the fourth century the growth was significant, comprising, according to some estimates, up to 10 percent of the population.[11] Accommodation by the empire was necessary, for the war on Christianity had failed miserably, dividing the populace. With the Edict of Toleration in AD 312 by Emperor Constantine, which recognized the Christian faith as a legal religion, and the Edict of Milan in AD 325 establishing Christianity as the official religion of the empire, the context of the Christian movement changed dramatically and permanently. With the change, the movement itself also changed dramatically and permanently. When the good of the empire included first the protection of the movement, then eventually the official promotion of the kingdom's ideals, the movement was tempted, as was Jesus, to adjust its orientation away from the promises of the kingdom of God and to orient itself just a little to the vertical pyramidal shape of the empire. But unlike Jesus, the leaders of the movement failed to recognize the dangers and resist the temptation.

Gradually and imperceptibly, the double adjustment occurred until the day when the conditions for full alignment existed. The shape of the empire and the shape of the kingdom were aligned. The church was now in the position to move, not forward toward the promises of the kingdom of God, but upward toward the top of the empire. From there the kingdom could use the coercive power of empire to successfully establish the kingdom in and of the empire.

The diagram below depicts these changes that began with Constantine's edicts, but were realized gradually and with periodic reversals.

11. Stark, *Cities of God*, 67.

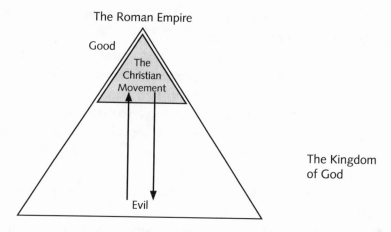

FIGURE 6.3. The Failure of Good in the Christian Movement

If the good of the empire is seen to approximate the goals of the kingdom, the movement's orientation and relationship to its culture changes dramatically over time. Gradually, imperceptibly, the Christian movement becomes "conformed to the patterns of the world" denounced by Paul (Rom 12:2a). Its identical shape allows it to fit in, to be a contributing part of the system that now protects it. It becomes increasingly hierarchical, organized to the point that it is a social institution with its own elite, its own official intellectuals, its very own disenfranchised, and a broad, stable base. Jesus might not be at the top of this pyramid, but his representatives, the rulers of both the church and the empire, are clearly there, representing Jesus' power and dominion. It is no longer a movement, vulnerable, prophetic, chaotic, and charismatic. It is no longer like Jesus in the world.

What changed for the Roman Empire in its "conversion"? The empire did not become less brutal, more equitable, more peaceful, and more just when it embraced Christianity officially. Rome did not begin to display the suffering and serving power of Jesus of Nazareth. Rather, Rome attempted to exercise the power and demonstrate the triumph of the risen, glorified Lord.

What about the church within the Roman Empire? Did the Christian movement that once displayed the power of the cross in the empire continue to do so? History shows that the Christian movement, not just the Roman Empire, was converted with the establishment of Christianity as the official religion of the empire. The Roman Empire became holy; the Christian movement became imperial.

It is not that the church deliberately abandoned its orientation toward the kingdom of God. Rather, the conditions under Constantine made it easy for the church to eventually confuse the kingdom of God with the Christian Roman Empire. As this occurred, the Christian movement, once a clear alternative to the oppressive and deadly social patterns of the empire, drifted upwards to the top of the pyramid where the power and the ability to control are concentrated.

This position of privilege, while seeming to signal triumph, was the opposite for the Christian movement in the Roman Empire. What would our world today be like if the Christian representatives of the kingdom in the empire would have continued to have been relegated to their original position lower on the pyramid, if they had never been tolerated or legal? What if the Christian movement had remained a kingdom-oriented movement instead of becoming an institution within and of the empire?

The evidence throughout history is that the permanent and universal temptation of humanity is as attractive for Christians as it is for people of all other religions or people of no religion. It is also just as destructive. For the Christian church in a world full of the power and the triumph of human achievement, the temptation to be as *gods* knowing good and evil becomes the temptation to be as *God* knowing good and evil. The desire for humans to achieve the power and triumph of the pagan gods or the God of the Scriptures is essentially indistinguishable in its effects on those who strive for it. Only the explanations, the justifications, and the theologies are different.

As in the empire, the organic intellectuals of the church, the charismatic leaders, those whose authority was earned by their demonstrable close relationship to Jesus in their lives, were replaced by traditional intellectuals, trained specialists with connections to the power of the elite families of the empire. These men—always men now—were no longer prophets; their voices replaced those of the pagan priests in legitimizing the evil of the empire for the cause of the kingdom. The kingdom of God was no longer present among but rather above the common people. It had arrived. It had conquered. It had converted the empire. Or perhaps it had been converted by the empire. Its authority came from the top down, just as in the empire. And just as in the empire, coercion and mystification became the tools of oppression rather than emancipation for those below. The names of the gods changed, but what the rulers of the empire began to do in the name of God was remarkably unchanged.

While the benefits for the elite were tremendous, the life of the lower classes did not improved greatly. Their pain, however, was ameliorated with the promise of future reward. Marx would correctly observe: "Religion is the sigh of the oppressed creature, the opiate of the people." Of course there were prophetic protests and voices of dissent, but now they were controlled by Christian rather than pagan promises, threats, and brutality.

Was the "triumph" of Christianity totally negative in the empire? Most certainly not. For an empire to become somewhat better through the influence of Christians is good. The problem is when Christians do not recognize that every human empire, even an empire that embraces Christianity as its official religion, is as much of a system of death as the Roman pagan system was. The empire cannot give life; it can only be more or less deadly for humans during their brief natural lives. The empire cannot give satisfaction, even with its ability to deliver huge quantities of everything imaginable to its citizens.

Powerful Christian nations since the Holy Roman Empire may vary in the level of brutality and evil that they commit in the name of Christ, but none of them, in spite of their lofty ideals, stirring religious justifications, and self-understanding as establishing Christ's rule in the world, none of them do so. "My kingdom," Jesus said, "is not from this world. If my kingdom were from this world my followers would be fighting" (John 18:36a). No matter what system of government, no matter how free and prosperous, no matter what deity is publicly worshipped or what percentage of the population is Christian, no nation or empire, large or small, is or ever will be the kingdom of God.

The temptation of the early Christian movement is the same temptation of all humanity, of Jesus, and of the church in the world today, especially in the empires perceived to be so good that they appear to be close to the kingdom.

Although the Roman Empire is history, empires live. It is another Christian empire, the United States of America, which currently exercises its power, demonstrates its achievements, and promotes its ideals throughout the world, to which we now turn. Empire now has global dimensions. It is on the global sea of pagan promises that Christian citizens of both empire and kingdom must navigate toward the kingdom.

7

Sailing the Global Pagan Sea

The Global Pagan Sea

As in the first century, the twenty-first-century world is like the sea. But a sea change is occurring. Human dissatisfaction, expectations, and hopes are rising around the world, especially in the poorer and developing nations, due partly to the relentless, image-mediated invasion of powerful, attractive pagan promises. A kind of global cultural warming is noticeable. Unforeseen and frightening "perfect storms" of social instability, economic tsunamis, and sometimes local waves of terror begin to build, also facilitated by social media technologies. The global pagan sea of human possibilities, promises, and peril is rising and traditional institutions, built for another climate, are threatened.

But, as in the current global warming debate, not everyone is convinced that globalization is changing anything of importance. Others applaud any evidence of change, believing above all in the potential of globalization for good. Some observers are alarmed at the perils of globalization, the potential disruption of traditional values, and shifts in the balance of trade, wealth, and power. Those concerned about globalization may seek to impede the plans for increased expansion of international trade. Still others see globalization as inevitable and believe that, regardless of whether it is positive or negative, there is nothing that can be done about it. One can neither escape globalization nor change its effects.

Is globalization really a greatly expanded, twenty-first-century version of the ancient pagan promises once promoted so successfully within the Roman Empire in the Mediterranean? And if it is, what are the implications for twenty-first-century Christians? What can we learn from Paul and the first-century Christian movement in the Mediterranean that will help us navigate globalization?

We begin with a general working definition of globalization. Globalization is generally understood to be the process of a worldwide diffusion of information and products made possible through highly developed technologies of communication and transportation. Additional features of globalization include mass migrations of people for economic reasons, and international trade agreements that create the conditions for the expansion of commerce across national boundaries. The digitally connected world makes possible the rapid and incessant trade of ideas and wealth that have implications for all human systems of knowledge and power including, politics, economics, religion, and science.

I am proposing another definition for consideration that focuses on the presuppositions, values, and goals inherent in globalization: *Globalization is the promotion of pagan promises of abundance in life to all people everywhere in the world.*

If this is an accurate summary of the "spirit" of globalization, several things become immediately clear. The promises of globalization contradict the promises of the kingdom; globalization is a powerful mission movement that competes with the mission movement of the kingdom of God; and all Christians everywhere will be affected by it in some way, with American Christians affected in particularly critical ways.

While a vast percentage of the world's population participates in the production and consumption of products designed to fulfill the pagan promises, the control of the design, promotion, and production of the promises and products is concentrated at the top of the pyramid. America and her Christian citizens are among the elite of this global empire. Globalization, then, is to American Christians what Romanization was to first-century Christians in the Mediterranean, especially those like Paul who were Roman citizens. This is a position of precarious privilege.

What are the pagan promises that Rome once promoted and displayed in the Mediterranean that are so enticing today? Pagan promises, as noted earlier, can be summed up as abundance in life. It is the promise of an abundance of the good, satisfying, rewarding, pleasurable, happy, and secure life that the pagan system offers. Peace, justice, wealth, health, beauty, individual freedom, self-gratification, pleasure, power, honor, domination of others, subjugation of enemies, delay of death, wisdom, status—the list seems to be everything humans desire and struggle to achieve. Are the promises realistic? What effects does pursuit of these promises have on those who believe them?

We return briefly to the Mediterranean and the Greek island of Samos, one of the islands Paul visited on his return voyage to Jerusalem at the end of his last missionary journey. Samos contains a remarkable aqueduct engineered by Eupalinus in the sixth century BC. The aqueduct is actually a tunnel through a small mountain, carved through solid rock. While all of the attention is given to the engineer, Eupalinus, for somehow figuring out how the workers could start tunneling from both ends and meet in the middle, the several groups of students whom I've taken to visit this tunnel are more impressed by the incredible amount of human labor it takes to hew a tunnel of just over a kilometer long (3,399 ft.) through solid rock.

Legend has it that this labor was done by slaves who were promised freedom upon completing the project. They could literally tunnel their way toward the promise of freedom, to life. In the meantime, they would be imprisoned inside the unfinished tunnel, toiling in near darkness toward the vision of the light of day, of liberty, and of happiness. But due to the deadly living and working environment inside the tunnel, none of the slaves made it to freedom. Motivated by the promise of freedom and life, they literally worked themselves to death inside their tunnel prison-grave of promise.

As in Rome, globalization holds the promise of abundance in life, but while some might achieve their dreams, and while most might see some progress in the direction of their longings, some limited fulfillment of these promises, neither Rome then nor globalization now can give life. Then as now, death could be delayed or ignored, but it could not be defeated. This awful truth, however, then as now, is somewhat ameliorated in the achievement of any noticeable progress toward the promises.

As in the Roman Empire, the struggle to achieve and maintain economic control never ends today. Globalization is marked by struggle and constant attempts to expand control. Globalization has features of a world war waged by America against her competitors for dominance, and with her partners to breach the barriers of all those parts of the planet that continue to resist their efforts to invade the market. The global war on terrorism and the simultaneous peace with friendly but brutal regimes is promoted as necessary to make the world safe. This safety includes the ability to trade with the rest of the world. The weapons employed by the political and business leaders in the nations at the top of the globalization pyramid are weapons of mass temptation, mass marketing, and mass consumption. Control is the goal. Massive profit is the reward.

Eventually, for those who disrupt and resist globalization, powerful weapons of destruction may be used, in far-off places like Iraq. Closer to home, fences must be built and patrolled in order to keep out those attracted by the tantalizing promise of abundance and who are desperate or hopeful enough to risk their lives attempting to achieve their dreams. Then as now, people risk their lives to achieve their promise-fueled dreams.

The quest by the powerful participants in the new global economic empire is for control and stability in the global marketplace in our sea-like world of human desires. Can this last? Is unlimited growth of the expectations, the markets, and the abundance of products sustainable? Is optimism warranted? Will globalization have a limited lifespan like every other form of empire before it?

The Roman Empire in the Mediterranean, an early form of globalization, ended. Tyre is another example a once-flourishing trade empire whose achievements and decline are described in Scripture. This once mighty Phoenician seaport is located in modern Lebanon. On the eastern end of the Mediterranean and linked to both the ancient land trade routes of the east and the seaports to the west, Tyre was ideally positioned to control trade. This it did very well, growing incredibly wealthy. Tyre dominated the sea trade, and figures so large in biblical and non-biblical history that the Mediterranean was sometimes referred to as the Tyrian

Sea. Jesus likely visited Tyre (Mark 7:31), as did Paul (Acts 21:3), something that brought me to Tyre as well almost two thousand years later.

Alexander the Great had besieged it in 332 BC, building an earthen causeway from the mainland to the island to get his great siege equipment across. A portion of the city of Tyre today is built on this causeway. The day I visited Tyre I sat on Alexander's now-urbanized causeway and read the prophet Ezekiel's description of Tyre, "which sits at the entrance to the sea, merchant of the peoples on many coastlands. . . . Your borders are in the heart of the seas; your builders made perfect your beauty. . . . [Many nations] did business with you out of the abundance of your great wealth" (Ezek 27:3a–4, 12a).

But Ezekiel's description of Tyre's wealth and control of trade does not end there. On the once formidable causeway I continued to read. "Now you are wrecked by the seas, in the depths of the waters; your merchandise and all your crew have sunk with you" (27:34). Glancing around, it was clear that Ezekiel's prediction had indeed occurred.

It is the way of all wealthy and powerful empires to decline and die, some violently and suddenly, others gradually, a kind of slow, steady decay as their wealth shrivels, their power and glory declines, and reckless, impassioned enemies who have been aggrieved or deprived gain momentum. The United States of America, having reached the height of its power and status in the world, is no exception. Like Tyre in Ezekiel's day, and Rome in Paul's, America in our day is losing its idealistic, youthful energy. Its wealth is being squandered. Its position of moral authority among nations continues to erode. America exercises her great power in increasingly desperate and contradictory ways as glory fades to greed.

America has never been, is not now, and never will be the kingdom of God. But while in the past there may have been a much greater consensus within the nation and around the world that America was an essentially Christian nation, the evidence that it is another of the world's great pagan empires is overwhelming. America is more like Rome than the biblical city on a hill, in spite of being a nation of remarkably active and committed Christians.

I want to emphasize here that I believe America to be, in comparison to other global empires of history, one of the best the world has ever seen. I realize that Christians of the British Empire felt the same, and they may have been right. Empires are not equally evil or good but can be relatively good or evil for their citizens in terms of fairness, justice, peace, and order. Empires can be relatively good and evil in terms of their foreign policy, their trade practices, their use of military, and their treatment of their enemies. Perhaps Christian empires are relatively better than pagan or secular empires or those of other religions or ideologies. The evidence is not always clear until the long-term effects of their policies and accomplishments become evident. What is clear is that Christian empires generally consider themselves to be better. They generally interpret their use of power to be justified on high moral principles. But no matter how relatively good an empire is, no empire ever has been or will ever be the kingdom of God.

America and the Global Empire

What Rome was in the Mediterranean, America has become in the world. While Rome assumed an endless expansion because of the superiority of the system of domination and control of human and material resources and aided by its superior military forces, America's rhetoric and actions indicate the same basic assumptions. The expansion of American influence is believed by Americans to be beneficial to others in the long run, even if not initially apparent to them. "Freedom," President Bush declared following the election in Iraq in January of 2005, "is on the march." Divine blessing and the related mandate to both spread the blessing and enjoy the benefits through both persuasion and force is assumed by many Americans, as it was by many in the Roman Empire.

This self-assurance of goodness that once energized the Roman Empire now enables America to consolidate diversity, organize energy, and control resources within its contested sphere of influence and domination. Both pagan and then Christian Rome in the past, and Christian America in the present, make their vaguely divine promises credible and attractive through their demonstrations of power and success far from home. Rome built and utilized a secure transportation system on land and sea. It maintained a reliable communications network and an effective administrative infrastructure. Rome exploited their allies and rewarded them for compliance. It conducted brutal military reprisals against any disruptive resistance or threat of it. Rome dominated the Mediterranean, displaying and demonstrating its unrivaled position continuously and defeating any challengers as often as necessary. The same list of accomplishments and characteristics enables America to dominate the world and to display and demonstrate its unrivaled, but increasingly challenged, superiority among nations.

The Roman system of control and domination throughout the Mediterranean was characterized by its ability to consolidate and protect the production and transportation of basic and luxury goods for maximum economic advantage to Rome. The accumulation of vast wealth through the control of trade and commerce enabled Rome to maintain its domination of the market and to extend its control on resources and trade through its engineering prowess, technological superiority, and cheap labor within the Mediterranean region.

With its wasteful, non-productive upper classes concentrated in Rome, there were plenty of goods for the elite, but far too little grain to feed the human population and the draft animals that provided the raw energy for the production of goods and services. This energy deficiency problem was solved by the great grain ships, the largest of their kind in the world at that time, that plied the Mediterranean constantly between Alexandria and Rome. The security and control of the grain-producing areas such as Egypt, and the shipping routes in the Mediterranean, were vital to the security and prosperity of Rome.[1] Grain was to Rome what oil is to America. Both grain fields and oil fields, the sources of energy, must be controlled.

The superior power of the Roman Empire in the Mediterranean eventually necessitated increasing displays and use of that power to prevent others from displacing Roman domination. As with Rome before, the awareness of this unique status of being the single superpower in the world and the desire to preserve that status indefinitely has lead American foreign policy and military strategy in the direction of what Noam Chomsky calls the "imperial grand strategy" of America in the

1. These great ships carried passengers as well. Paul utilizes two grain ships on his voyage to Rome. These ships are mentioned and described as being from Alexandria, on their way to Rome (Acts 27:6 and 28:11). For extensive research on Mediterranean shipping in the Roman Empire, including the grain trade between Rome and Egypt, see Casson's *Travel*, 149–62; and *Mariners*, 206–12.

world. This strategy is "the declared intention of the most powerful state in history to maintain its hegemony through the threat or use of military force, the dimension of power in which it reigns supreme."[2]

A combination of fear of the enemy, sense of superior moral status, and effectiveness of the military to provide security ensured that the inhabitants of the Roman Empire willingly supported or at least tolerated the enormous costs of maintaining an army that could overwhelmingly defeat its weaker and smaller enemy nations or peoples.[3] The same can be said of America. In Rome, as in America at many points in her history, peace was defined by the utter destruction of the enemy. Justice was not so much the issue; absence of violent resistance was. Under threat, security trumps justice, human rights, and civil liberties in the regions of military conflict in which Rome or America is involved.

In both the Roman Empire and America today, the nurturing and exploitation of fear by the ruling elite is often assisted by gullible or cynical—it hardly matters which—religious leaders, and others with public influence. Fear was and is effective in mobilizing the level of popular support necessary for overcoming resistance to the staggering human, spiritual, moral, and economic costs of wars of any kind, both in the Roman Empire and America.

Rome's domination of the Mediterranean world was successful not simply because of its military capabilities, its brutal repression of all enemies, its control of trade, and its effective organization. Rome's visible power and triumph throughout the Mediterranean made the promises of the pagan gods somehow credible, immediate, and attractive. The cultural domination of Rome in the Mediterranean created the conditions of willing cooperation, for the rewards of "buying into" the Roman system were far greater and more likely to be attained than by resisting Rome and its pagan promises.

However, Rome's cultural influence in the Mediterranean pales beside the sheer enormity of the American power and influence in the

2. Chomsky, *Hegemony*, 11.

3. The promotion and exploitation of fear for political and economic reasons pervades public rhetoric. There are both political and monetary rewards for those who control not only the good news of the market through the media, but the bad news of the world, especially of the threat to America by its enemies. "It is not easy . . . to maintain political power. Only one good method is known: inspire fear" (ibid., 115).

entire world. The conditions for an expanding free market, dominated by America for the benefit of her corporate and political elite and to a lesser extent her citizens, is global. Indeed the world is seen, through the eyes of international corporations, as a global market. Its peoples are potential consumers of goods and services produced by America and her economic partners. On one hand, human rights, justice, and equality are defined in terms of free market theories. On the other hand, human rights may be ignored if favorable trade relations that allow maximum corporate profit are threatened. Thus, security has to do not with the internal security of the residents of embarrassingly brutal regimes with whom America trades everything from armaments to zippers, but rather with concerns about any threats to the security of investments, uninterrupted production, and conditions for maximum consumption.

America dominates the global entertainment market.[4] With its combination of free speech, creativity, and financial resources to invest, America has the conditions for cultural domination through its entertainment industry, even in areas where free speech is not present. Any nation that seeks to restrict the intrusion of American entertainment runs the risk of an American challenge of its restrictions on human rights; in this case, the right to be manipulated and seduced by unlimited pagan promises.

America develops trade relations with certain brutal regimes and wages war on others under the lofty banners of security, peace, democracy, and liberation.[5] The argument that these trade agreements with brutal regimes is good for American self-interest is cultivated by national leaders. However, when it becomes clear that it is actually the self-interests of the investors and corporations within the global marketplace that are being satisfied, this argument becomes less effective to rally support among the American populace. Fear of economic decline then needs to be elevated enough to minimize public concern about the lack of democracy or abuses of human rights among trading partners.

The world of consumers needs both dissatisfaction and stability if the market is to expand and reach its full potential. The creative genius of

4. In *Jihad,* Barber documents American dominance in the world of film, television, music, and print media. See pp. 88–136.

5. For a litany of historic examples, see Chomsky, *Hegemony,* 109–43.

American marketing can provide both the dissatisfaction and the products that seem to temporarily satisfy them, while the American military and its military partners can provide the necessary stability.

Manipulation of youth who are told, "you can be what you chose" in a world of ambiguous morality, meaning, and purpose, can generate unlimited profit for those who control the youth market. Creative, entertaining, and relentless marketing produces and propagates images that create dissatisfaction. Products that promise to fill the vacancies, the dread, the disappointment, and the disillusionment not only of the youth, but everyone in a youth-obsessed culture, are offered. By making consumers out of everyone, creating desires and transforming "wants" to "needs," then offering products that promise to fulfill those desires, wants, and needs, the profit climbs.

Christian citizens of America not only benefit along with everyone else, they experience the same dissatisfaction, and buy the same products that promise to give them beauty, wealth, security, health, and happiness. Christians and pagans, the holy and the hedonistic, hope in the promises and consume the products. *E pluribus unum* may not describe the experience of everyone in American society, but it applies to those who participate in the global marketplace in America and around the world.

How remarkably similar are the definitions and demonstrations of the good life by the elite in the Roman Empire to those promoted today within the American marketplace and around the world! How productive! How profitable! How pagan!

Not everyone is happy within the pagan marketplace, but everyone is content, it seems, with sharing some of the benefits of its power and profitability—even the church.[6] The silversmiths in Ephesus would not feel threatened by the church of America. They would simply produce, along with pagan products to be promoted through the media and sold

---

6. While it is true that certain products are rightly identified and resisted by some American Christians and organizations as being evil (pornography, graphic violence, or blasphemy in entertainment, for example) the consumption patterns of Christians do not seem to be noticeably different from that of the rest of society. What is amazing is not the apparent unconcern Christians at the relentless promotion of all pagan values and products, but the fact that their faith does not seem to affect their own consumption patterns or the successful promotion of those pagan values and products, both in America and from America to the rest of the ends of the earth.

in Walmart, crosses and angels to be sold in the Christian bookstore next door.

This marketing of the original sin is succeeding, not only by making the world safe for the promotion of pagan products for a profit, but by making the Christians of America reluctant to be prophetic. It is successful because the definitions of the abundant life of the kingdom have been co-opted and distorted by the pagan/Christian culture of America, and because cooperation allows the church to share in the power and success of the nation.

Whereas Rome's promotion of the pagan system necessitated massive investments in the demonstration of its power and success, today the images of success and achievement are transmitted globally through low-cost digital images. This assures global saturation in the guise of freedom of information, the personal right for everyone to know what they are missing and what they need to have in order to be fulfilled. Let's look at the message of the medium.

Individualism is both inherent in the medium and the message. The Internet for example, gives the consumer incredible control over what he or she wishes to know, to observe, and to consume. It is as if the entire world of possibilities is immediately and individually at the fingertips of any human with a device connected to the Internet. The ability to peruse and explore, to surf the sea of information, promises, and products, is unprecedented. Whereas the Mediterranean Sea provided the linkage to the babble of options around the Mediterranean, the Internet now carries the images, promises, and products directly to each individual.

The digital entertainment industry produces what Barber calls "infotainment,"[7] extended commercial messages that glorify everything from violence, sexual license, domination, and self-gratification to power, wealth, and beauty. The messages are at once shocking and enticing, dividing traditional societies between age groups, inciting desire, envy, and hatred among the youth, especially young male populations, and particularly among those who are unemployed, humiliated, and disenfranchised.

The proliferation of information sources accessible around the world both on the Internet and on television enables individuals to select the messages they desire to consume. Information itself, including interna-

7. See Barber *Jihad*, 64–65.

tional news, must be marketed in order to attract consumers. This information market drives the news networks around the world. It is now possible to watch the news you want to hear and, alarmingly, to ignore and dismiss that which conflicts with what you want to believe. Good-hearted Americans, Christians among them, can support evil defined as good, for the information sources they have selected interpret events in such a way that supports and strengthens the national myth of American righteousness, even in its brutal wars. All of this can be seen as the global marketing of paganism in digital form.

Even a cursory perusal of the printed promises for personal power and status, luridly displayed on any large magazine stand in America and in international markets around the world, reveals that beauty, health, wealth, success, and enjoyment are the primary themes. While far less invasive and accessible, printed products, often produced by the same corporations that own the digital media, reveal the pagan character of the global market. This could be seen as the marketing of paganism in printed form.

Pluralism of truth is not only a feature of the global information market, but is promoted as a value. The freedom to choose everything from goods to gods, from lifestyles to abortion and assisted suicide, is promoted as an essential human right by those who profit from the proliferation of options. Restrictions on individual freedom, especially when these restrictions are based on appeals to religious authority, are relentlessly denounced or demeaned by producers of consumer products of all kinds.[8]

While the American global marketing empire espouses individual freedom of choice, and while freedom of religion is at the heart of the American concept of individual freedom, religion can be somewhat of a problem in the global market. The elite of the global marketing empire publicly claim to respect the freedom to choose a particular religion, but because religion historically has sometimes negatively affected the consumption patterns of its adherents, the freedom to choose not to be restrained by "tradition" is promoted. Everyone, according to the marketers, has the right to choose or not to choose their own interpretations

---

8. Consumer products in this Information Age include "cultural products" such as values, ideals, dreams, fears, worldviews, religions, and ideologies, as well as items such as cosmetics, fashion, liposuction, and BMWs.

of religious restrictions. This message seems to be more effective among some religions than others. Religion can provide either contentment with what one already has or prohibitions against acquiring what is offered in the global market. Both are detrimental to consumption.

Thus, representatives of religions who support the cultural values of consumption or individual freedom of choice are regularly given a more favorable image in the media than those who advocate positions counter to the values of the market. Religions that directly oppose the pagan values of the market are feared, ridiculed, and undermined, such as in the case of Islam.

Are the values of the kingdom and those of the empire really the same? While the global marketing strategies do not entice many Christians around the world to deliberately abandon their faith in Jesus and to place it in the pagan promises of the marketplace, there is a tendency to begin to view God from a consumer's point of view. Like choosing which news source to believe, one can choose the definitions of God with which one is comfortable. The pluralism of the global market extends to the church, and Jesus is measured by his ability to fulfill a believer's desires for status, enjoyment, wealth, and health in comparison to other products that promise to do the same thing. In the consumer-oriented climate of the global market, Jesus may be one of many life-enhancing promises that are believed. This is can be viewed as the marketing of pagan pantheism.

The global market pushes consumers in the direction of openness to anything that works. What works is right and justifiable. The question consumers of religious products may begin to ask is not so much whether a religious claim is true, but whether it accomplishes what it promises to do. While truth and effectiveness are not necessarily contradictory features, truth is often more difficult than effectiveness to verify. An ultimately false claim might work well on the surface, or temporarily deliver what it promises, as did the temptation of Adam and Eve in the Garden. Truth might not appear to be effective; for instance, does Jesus' command to "love your enemies" work? It depends on the criteria. This is a practical, pragmatic paganism.

Education and English-language fluency enables participation and reward in the global marketing empire dominated by American self-interest. Both education and English fluency promise access to power, the avenue to status, and the road to success. Parents in poorer countries will make incredible sacrifices, working endless hours and denying themselves of anything above their basic needs, in order to send their children away for a Western education. Youth from poorer nations will leave family and friends for years at a time, perhaps never to return, in order to study in the West. Once there, they may work endless hours to master the English language, achieve high grades, and to earn, sometimes illegally, enough money to live on.

But knowledge truly is power in the global economy and opens the doors for participation in the rewards of globalization. Although the rewards are often elusive and only partially fulfill the expectations and dreams, to participate even on lower levels in globalization is far more rewarding than not participating at all. How different is this than slavery in the Roman Empire, with the perpetual promise of freedom and perhaps even citizenship, goals that enabled the citizen to one day at last enjoy the fruit of a lifetime of labor? This can be seen as the power and promise of paganism in linguistic and academic forms.

In the global pagan marketing empire, the sculpted images of the gods that functioned to connect the individual to the power of the unseen gods are today replaced by personal, powerful, tiny digital devices such as smart phones, iPods, and e-readers with instant access to the Internet. These miniature devices connect the individual to the seemingly infinite power of the knowledge of good and evil in the human universe. This connectedness to the unseen world of knowledge provides those who possess the devices to share in the power of human achievements. Connection to the Internet gives access to the complete range of human creativity, imagination, and knowledge of good and evil much as the pantheon of pagan gods from Aphrodite to Zeus. Like the pagan gods, this power makes no moral demands, only promises. Through digital technologically, the Tree of Knowledge of Good and Evil is always available. The devices themselves are status symbols.

Could this miniaturization of knowledge power also influence how Christians in America imagine God? The God of Scripture must now compete with the gods of personal digital devices, these personal, miniature, instantaneous, and powerful devices that instantly help us meet our incessant demands. These gods, in our technologically enhanced human imagination, are the pagan gods created in human image. The God of Scripture can be viewed, along with our electronic gadgets, as a source of personal power, a resource for life, but not *the* source of life. We could call this the technologically enhanced theology of paganism.

There is a darker, more violent side to globalization and the American church's participation in its power and its quest for continued success. An example of the perversion of kingdom values by Christian elite is especially evident in the rhetoric and actions of the ongoing war on terror of recent administrations, which justifies occupation of countries such as Afghanistan and Iraq. The strategic marketing of fear in order to globalize the ongoing war on terror has been effective among significant portions of American Christian churches.

What is the nature of this fear that overcomes the church and enables it to justify completely anti-Christian responses to evil? Is it the fear of terrorists? The fear of losing the privilege of American power and status in the world? Is it the fear of the unknown, of chaos, of the sea? Paul's instructions to "overcome evil with good" seem totally irrelevant and ineffective as a national policy for a Christian nation in combating evil (Rom 12:21).[9] So while love may indeed overcome fear (1 John 4:18), love for the enemy does not seem to make one safe, and is not an obviously effective strategy for institutional and national self-preservation.

The Church in America

The official myths of America that sustain and integrate our culture include the notion that the nation was founded by a people who were oppressed and disadvantaged by the corrupt cooperation of church and state in Europe. Their exodus was not from the slavery of Egypt, but from the religious repression and restrictions of Europe. Like the Israelites, our

---

9. The familiar passage in Romans 13 that, "every person must be subject to the governing authorities, for there is no authority except from God," is taken by many Christians to mean support for even those policies that are reprehensible for Christians, especially if their leaders claim to be Christian. Space does not permit an extensive discussion of alternative understandings of this passage. For a careful counterargument against Christian acquiescence to evil done in the name of God by government, see Yoder' *Politics of Jesus*, in particular his treatment of what it means to "be subject" in his chapter on Romans 13, pp. 193–214.

ancestors were a righteous people, ordained by God to inhabit the "land of promise," establishing, as it were, a new kingdom of God in the new world. The indigenous population, like the Canaanites in the Promised Land, needed to be subdued and driven out. The lofty vision of being a chosen and blessed nation establishing righteousness, justice, and freedom in the world, a beacon of hope, a city set on the hill, a light to the nations, was solidly grounded in scriptural images. God was with America from the very beginning.[10]

The Declaration of Independence, drafted by Thomas Jefferson, with its vaguely Christian ideals and scriptural inferences, enshrines the self-understanding of America's role as establishing the will of the Creator in the American national experiment. "All men," Jefferson wrote in the remarkably moving document, "are endowed by the Creator with inalienable rights, among which are the right of life, liberty, and pursuit of happiness." While the phrase "pursuit of happiness," undefined and unqualified as it is, may have been a poor choice of words,[11] this formula of three essential God-given rights are words that comprise the heart of the sacred myth of American self-understanding and its divine call that shapes its domestic policy and sense of mission in the world.

Thomas Jefferson is also credited with crafting the Bill of Rights, the group of Amendments added to the Constitution in 1791. Religion is on the very top of the list. The First Amendment states: "Congress shall make no law respecting an establishment of religion, or prohibiting the free exercise thereof; or abridging the freedom of speech, or of the press; or the right of people peaceably to assemble, and to petition the Government in redress of grievances."

A second deeply imbedded image in the American mentality from very early on is also a phrase coined by Thomas Jefferson. The "wall of separation" Jefferson advocated in his letter in 1802 to the Danbury Baptist Association in Connecticut, a minority religious group there, states: "Religion is a matter which lies solely between man and his God;

10. Hutchison, in his book *Errand*, traces this central assumption in American self-understanding.

11. What is happiness and how can it be achieved? This right has created the right of unlimited desire and the right of the marketplace to achieve satisfaction. This right, when extended to the world, views the people of the world as consumers of products for their happiness, the right to have access to Walmart and MTV via satellite.

that he owes account to none other for his faith or his worship; that the legislative powers of the Government reaches actions only and not opinions . . . [government] should make no law respecting the establishment of religion, or prohibiting the free exercise thereof, thus building a wall of separation between Church and State." This quote has since become a kind of sacred ideal that goes beyond the words of the First Amendment.

While the divine blessing and calling of America embedded in its national myth is not unique among Christian empires, the principle of the non-establishment of religion and the wall of separation between church and state, seems to be a necessary improvement, mitigating against the corruption of concentrated power and the selfish acquisition of it by both the churches and the government of America. While legally this has prevented the church from directly exercising its power through the instruments of power of the state, it has not prevented the church from assuming a role of national moral guardian, or of being a voluntary ally or handmaiden of the wealthy and the powerful in America.

Effective national leaders in America recognize the importance of religion in shaping public support for otherwise morally reprehensible policies. Support from the church for the policies of the rulers is especially important in a democracy. "Controlling the general population has always been a dominant concern of power and privilege," Chomsky writes, but because "coercion was a tool of diminishing utility" in modernity, religious resistance to public policy that contradicts moral sensibilities needs to be redirected, "primarily through control of opinion and attitude."[12] Thus, the powerful leaders of democracies need to persuade the powerful leaders of religion that their political platform and public policies are beneficial to their churches and their agendas. The "control of opinion is the foundation of government, from the most despotic to the most free. . . . It is far more important in the more free societies, where obedience cannot be maintained by the lash."[13]

If the religious leaders are convinced of this, they may seek to persuade the adherents of their respective religions to vote for candidates who reflect and support their own religious values. Once elected, the decisions of the political leaders are less likely to be criticized and challenged

12. Chomsky, *Hegemony*, 5–6.
13. Ibid., 7.

by their supporters and more likely to be interpreted as good. The wall of separation only separates in terms of official ties. It does not separate influence and power. It does not separate gratitude and voting patterns. It does not separate the rewards of voluntary and mutually beneficial cooperation of church and state.

The wall of separation does not prevent a blurring of the distinctions between empire and kingdom. One of the two slogans that adorn American coinage, *E pluribus unum* ("out of many, one"), associated with the successful integration of vastly diverse peoples into one empire, is an ideal of both America and the kingdom of God. The other slogan, "in God we trust," parallels the pagan assumption that the goodness and success of the Roman Empire was both contingent upon and a demonstration of divine favor. The official nod to the gods, the public displays of loyalty, the temples on the hills and harbors, and the private devotion to those gods who promised the most of what one desired, all helped to consolidate and unify the diverse peoples of the empire for the good of the empire.

The incredible power of America's wealth is shared by those who possess any amount of its currency, whether citizens or non-citizens, rich or poor. The slogan may not be personally shared by everyone who possesses the currency, but the association of the wealth of the nation with God's blessing and favor that is implied by the slogan is satisfying for many Americans. For Christians, the slogan is yet another reassurance of good intentions, the public nod to the God they privately worship, that their God is the God of the nation and is associated with the abundance they enjoy.

Public monuments such as the Statue of Liberty symbolize the righteous ideals and the values of the American Promised Land. The Statue of Liberty, donated by the French government in 1886, which provided inspiration to the "poor, the huddled masses" entering New York harbor, is one of the most important. This thoroughly secular, yet vaguely religious symbol of goodness has the function of heroic monuments and pagan temples dominating the areas around and above the harbors of the Mediterranean in the first century. It is both a promise and a symbol of hope, partly experienced, but seldom fully, by the majority of those who arrive with their hope, dreams, and expectations.

The myths of divine origin, blessing, and mission in the world are thus integrated into the ethos, self-understanding, and self-importance of America through slogans and symbols. There is however, a problem. The actions of America, the domestic and foreign policies of the governments elected by her citizens, many of whom are publicly Christians, not only contradict the teachings of Jesus, they contradict America's own ideals and promises of liberty and justice for all internally, and the means of promoting these ideals elsewhere. In this respect America is similar to all empires, especially to the Roman Empire.

The diagram below depicts the results of succumbing to the irresistible upward lure for the good church of good America.

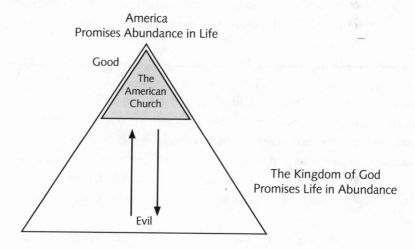

FIGURE 7.1. The Position of the Church in America

But who can blame the church for accepting an invitation to share in the power and control at the top, not only of the American nation, but at the top of the world? When the elite of the nation and the elite of the church work together, is this not better than when the national rulers oppose the church? Is it not possible to make the world a better place from this position and perhaps even share the good news of the kingdom more effectively? Yet, history demonstrates that when the church is confused with the kingdom of God, and the kingdom is confused with the empire or nation, it may benefit the nation in reaching its goals, but it certainly does not help the church on its voyage of faith toward the kingdom.

American Christians, like the Christians in the post-Constantine Roman Empire, are always in danger of confusing the empire or nation with the kingdom of God. The original sin of the Christian movement was not that it succeeded in changing the Roman Empire as the movement grew to a critical mass, but that it moved toward the top at the invitation of Constantine. The confusion of empire and kingdom is the permanent and universal temptation for all Christians, but is especially attractive to Christians in America, with rulers who, like Constantine, acknowledge their faith publicly. The temptation is to build some kind of socially acceptable organization that elevates the status and increases the power and security of the church. The security of our national economic system becomes the church's security.

However, the rising level of the pagan sea is threatening the security of religious institutions built to meet the contingencies of another time and place, when American Christians viewed matters of faith as being individual, simple, and local choices. What are the options for that great traditional institution, the American church, firmly built on American cultural assumptions, but near the edge of the sea, when that sea begins to wash away its firm foundations, to lap at its threshold, to seep into the sanctuary, to corrode the symbols once thought to be made of stainless steel?

Should the church retreat to higher grounds of tradition? Should we build theological dikes and levees to resist the encroaching waters? Should we perhaps call on and expect help from above, the helicopters of the celestial Coast Guard for dramatic rescue? Or should we adapt and conform as we are swept out to sea? While these are all possibilities, none are modeled by Jesus, and certainly not by Paul and the early Christian movement in the Mediterranean, according to Acts. And while all of these possibilities could potentially save the church as an institution from drowning in a pagan sea, it is the isolation from or absorption into the sea that makes these choices contradictory to Jesus' directive and Paul's example.

Like Paul we are citizens of an empire that controls the world for now. Like Paul we are also citizens of the kingdom of God. Like Saul, we need a conversion, for it is also hard for us to continue to seek our own security, to control society, and to confuse empire and kingdom when we succeed. It is hard for us to kick against the goads of our own cultural captivity in the most powerful and glorious and arguably the best pagan/Christian empire in the history of the world. What can American Christians in the midst of globalization learn from Paul in the Roman Empire?

We need to learn, as the early Christian movement in the Mediterranean did, to sail the pagan sea, to use this sea without being inundated by it, and to navigate this perilous sea with confidence toward the promises of the kingdom. We need to learn to leave our self-created stability for the vulnerability of following Jesus. We need to learn to utilize the storms of the sea-like world and internal tensions aboard the ship-like church in order to move toward the kingdom of God. For to the extent that we American Christians let go of our control, power, and success, we will experience and share, not abundance in life, but the life of abundance Jesus promised those who follow him.

We must go down to the sea again.

8

On the Voyage toward the Kingdom

Conversion

IT WAS NOT EASY to travel from Israel to Syria in early 2005. To do so required some creative evasion of the enforcers of Syrian policy, which prohibits anyone who has visited Israel or, as named on the Syrian visa application, "the illegally occupied Palestinian territories," to enter their beautiful country. With a "clean" passport and a Syrian visitor's visa I had obtained when we were in the United States over Christmas, I was ready. The journey of 250 miles took 12 hours—a bus from the Ashkelon marina to the airport at Tel Aviv, a short flight from Tel Aviv to Amman, Jordan, a taxi to central Amman, and finally a *service* (shared taxi) from Amman to Damascus.

My hosts in Damascus were exceptionally gracious, as were the many Syrians I met. I discussed the Apostle Paul with Patriarch Zakka of the Syrian Orthodox Church and with Patriarch Ignatius of the Greek Orthodox Church. I walked Straight Street and visited the sites of Ananias's house and Saul's famous basket-over-the-wall escape. A traditional site of Saul's conversion, Kawkab, was the highlight. The old Roman road rises slightly at the site and one can catch the first glimpse of Damascus ahead to the north, and, looking southwest, view the snowy profile of Mt. Hermon. It is a peaceful and marvelous spot and I lingered with my hosts in the shade, drinking tea served by Father Matta, the resident monk, discussing the ancient story and the impact of Saul's conversion on the history of the West.

On the following day I left Damascus for Jordan and then back across the Allenby Bridge into Israel. It happened to be Easter morning. The sun had just risen as our *service* pulled out of sleeping Damascus and headed down the road toward Amman. The car was packed and the passengers made attempts at conversation across the language barriers. I discovered the driver was Syrian. A Druze man who had fled his village on the Golan in the 1973 Syrian war with Israel was riding in the front seat. Next to me in the back was a married couple from Fallujah, Iraq, refugees living in Syria. Their home, they explained, was destroyed by the American bombing during the Gulf War.

Try to imagine if you can, what it was like to be the only American passenger in that car under such circumstances. Syrian, Iraqi, and American, Muslim, Druze, and Christian, tightly packed together in a small car for four hours on the Damascus road. But I was surprised and overwhelmed by the good nature of the passengers, especially of the Iraqis, as they described their shattered lives and gently explained why the Americans are so resented in the Middle East.

I thought of Saul, a Roman citizen, on the Damascus road. I introduced Saul and his nearby conversion briefly when they asked why I was in Syria.

"Isn't it some kind of Christian holiday today?" the Iraqi man asked after listening to the story of Saul meeting Jesus.

"Yes, it's Easter."

"What happened on Easter?"

"Jesus' resurrection." I had never been asked that question before.

We continued to talk about suffering and hope, evil and Easter, life and death, until we reached Amman. The next day an email was waiting from "your Iraqi friend." I opened it. "Happy Easter!" it said.

I will never forget traveling the Damascus road and the conversation with those Muslim refugees about Saul's conversion and Jesus' resurrection. I wish all American Christians could travel the Damascus road with Saul and with Iraqi refugees from our war in Iraq.

Like Saul, we Christians in America may believe ourselves to be making real progress building the kingdom. We may feel we are doing God's work in the world as we busily travel to and from Baghdad, Wheaton, Rome, New York, or Los Angeles. Like Saul, we may see the United States of America and its Christian citizens as God's special representatives in the world, battling all manner of evil, from terror to tyranny, from dictators to drugs. Like Saul we may support and be supported by the self-serving, often hypocritical, and sometimes destructive foreign policies of the American government within globalization, and the inequitable and shortsighted domestic policies that protect the rich at the expense of the poor.

"But America is the envy of the world, it does so much right, the system works quite well," you might say, and you would be right. Both the world's poor and the world's upwardly mobile envy America. I want to acknowledge as well that, comparatively speaking, there *is* so much America has done and continues to do right from the perspective of the values of the kingdom of God. For this we should be grateful, but our gratitude should never translate into support of any evil, which America has demonstrated clearly it is capable of doing, as have all other nations in history.

Not only do we American Christians sometimes give tacit or active support to some of the "necessary evil" of America's actions in the world, we support the "good" of the system that promotes pagan promises of abundance in life in the global market. We may not be aware of the consequences and effects of our nation's power for good and evil in the world. We may not understand how America and American Christians are viewed in the rest of the world. However, our lack of knowledge about the world, America, and American Christianity within the context of globalism is no excuse for participating in and supporting pagan evil or pagan good, even that which is done in the name of God. We American Christians can be convinced, like Saul, that we are doing the work of God in the world while actually doing the opposite.

Saul was concerned with the survival of Judaism within the Roman Empire, surrounded as it was by paganism, creeping Hellenization, and the cooperation of corrupt Jewish authorities with the Roman rulers. What seems to have been particularly troublesome for Saul was the radically inclusive movement of Jesus, which was especially popular among the poor and unlearned. But he was sincerely fighting the wrong battle, against the wrong enemy, for the wrong reasons. In the process, he misunderstood and misrepresented the God whom he thought he was serving. American Christians can unwittingly do the same.

Like Saul, we need an encounter with the crucified and living Lord of all, an encounter that reveals to us the reality of the kingdom and our own misguided zeal. We American Christians need conversion.[1]

It is not so much that American Christians need to become political and social activists for reform, prophetically speaking out against the promotion and profit from the pagan patterns of good and evil committed by America in the world. That would be welcome, but as a first step toward Jesus and the kingdom, and away from our embrace of our nation's self-serving national agenda in the world, we American Christians simply need to stop supporting evil in the world, no matter who commits it, for any reason.

It is for reasons of representing the good news of Jesus authentically that American Christians need conversion. Saul was misrepresenting the God he desired to serve. When we American Christians support false and evil facets of American policy, we are misrepresenting Jesus to the rest of the world. We need conversion for the sake of Jesus' reputation in the world.

Saul's conversion was from the power of a religious system of good and evil to the power of the cross and the resurrection. Neither the power of reward or punishment in the Roman system nor the power of the promises and threats in the Jewish system controlled Saul following his encounter with Jesus. We, the American church, need to be delivered from both the enticement of success and the fear of the decline of our institutions. We American Christians need to be liberated from our fear of the evil of terrorism, of social chaos, or of anything that motivates Christians and others to support and justify evil means that promise a good end. Because Jesus' resurrection makes our self-preservation unnecessary, evil committed for self-preservation or the preservation of the church is also unnecessary. There is no necessary evil for Jesus or his followers. American

---

1. Wallis's book *Conversion* makes a compelling case for thinking of the radical change of direction needed for the American church.

policy thrives on the cultivation of fear. Perfect fear casts out love. The cross demonstrates the opposite—the triumph of love over fear.

Saul's conversion changed his understanding of authority. Saul's authority had originated from Jerusalem. Now he was on his way to Damascus with his dubious letters authorizing his violence against the Christians there. Jesus also had given authority to his apostles in Jerusalem, but confronted Saul at the eastern edge of the empire, where he met and recognized the preeminence of Jesus' authority. Although he occasionally returned to Jerusalem following his conversion, Saul never returned there seeking authorization. Power and authority in the kingdom of God, unlike in empires, has no capital. Authority comes from relating to Jesus, not Jerusalem, Rome, or Washington, DC. American Christians, like Saul, need a conversion in our understanding of power and authority.

Saul's conversion changed his religious status in Judaism and his social status in the empire. He released his grasp of the status possible within religion and empire and embraced the shame of the cross, the most shameful symbol of defeat in the empire. Like Saul, American Christians share the status of a powerful empire in the world. Like Saul, we need a conversion from being enamored by the success of our capitalist system in the world to the triumph of the crucified and risen Lord.

Conversion is the beginning of the voyage toward the kingdom, but not the end. Conversion is a radical change of direction in life, which may take, because of history and momentum, a long period of time to implement and demonstrate to others. But, as in sailing, orientation eventually determines progress toward the destination. Saul's orientation in life changed on the Damascus road. He began to follow the crucified and risen Lord in the empire toward the kingdom, all the way to Rome.

Conversion changed Saul's social identity from that of an emerging leader in the anti-Christian reactionary movement to that of an apostle of the Christian movement. Conversion that changes our identity is as necessary for American Christians as for Saul. But, as Saul discovered, conversion is costly. Will the business elite applaud if American Christians began to threaten and undermine the pagan market because people do not need their products anymore? Will the political elite rejoice when Christians do not support self-serving national policies that are accompanied or achieved by war? Will the cultural elite be grateful for Christians who speak out against socially acceptable prejudice, erosion of moral values, or neglect of the poor? Not likely.

We need a change of self-identity from considering ourselves superior to Christians in other parts of the world such as France, Palestine, or Iraq. At one time, Saul thought of himself to be better than both the Christians and the pagans. But following his conversion he called himself the "least of the Apostles" (1 Cor 15:9). Could American Christians be converted to humility and the ability to identity with others they deem inferior or mistaken, as was Saul?

The final feature of Saul's conversion was his commission as an apostle. Saul understood his commission to preach the gospel to the Gentiles and his authority to represent Jesus to the world as grounded in his encounter with Jesus (Acts 26:12–20). Saul's unwavering commitment to Jesus, to his commissioning, and to the pagan world was absolute. Once Saul had seen Jesus, no threat or reward by Roman or Jewish authorities was effective in changing Saul's commitments.

Conversion for Saul was a change in his view of empire, the kingdom of God, his identity, his orientation in life, his status, his power and authority, his direction, and his agenda. All of this changed in his encounter with Jesus. It is this kind of conversion that we American Christians also need.

Citizens of Empire and Kingdom

Paul experienced both the benefits and burdens of being a Roman citizen as a citizen of the kingdom of God. While we American Christians share this distinct feature of Paul's dual citizenship, living in a democracy with Christian roots and values complicates any easy comparisons to Paul. Would Paul urge American Christians to develop civic responsibility, to vote, or even to run for elected office? While it is not possible here to adequately address this issue that has divided Christians into warring political camps and has caused other Christians to withdraw from the political arena entirely, I'll offer several basic principles implied in Paul's writings to Christians of the empire.

Paul is very familiar with the mistakes, the lifestyles, and the sins of pagans. Yet he never expects pagans to be less pagan or to try to act like he expects Christians to live. Paul spends no time at all trying to get pagans to do so. Paul does, however, expect Christians to stop acting like pagans. His directions, advice, and scolding about behavior are focused on Christians, not pagans.

Christians in America should focus their attention on being authentic followers and representatives of Jesus in the world and to call all other American Christians to do the same, rather than attempting to impose Christian values on modern pagans and their practices in American society. After all, if the majority of Americans are Christians, as polls indicate, society would be transformed by the gospel lived out by Christians! While prophetic witness and even protest against any injustices and evils in society would likely be something Paul would see as legitimate for Christians, he would also find attempts to impose Christian values on non-Christians through the exercise of coercive power as contradicting the teachings and example of Jesus.

Voting is another issue Paul did not have to address. Would Paul encourage American Christians to "vote their conscience?" Perhaps. I would suggest that Paul would not encourage Christians to simply vote for candidates who promise what Christians want exclusively for themselves, but for candidates whose policies are fair and just for the non-Christians, for the strangers and foreigners among us, and for the poor around the world. The more Christian a candidate claims to be, the more consistently that candidate would have to demonstrate Christ-likeness in his or her policies if Paul were to endorse that candidate. Paul would not encourage American Christians primarily to vote for candidates who promise privilege and special protection especially for Christians.

But there are other features of the privileges of American citizenship to which Paul's example and writings relate more directly. Freedom, wealth, and status are benefits of both Roman and American citizenship and are issues Paul faced personally and observed in the churches he started.

Being a citizen of a nation dominant in the global empire provides incredible freedom to travel almost everywhere in the world and protection as we do so. Our American citizenship also provides us with a high status when we find ourselves among admirers of America, and awkwardness when among America's detractors. Our American passport allows us to choose destinations freely and to leave quickly. The international connections Americans enjoy almost everywhere in the world give us access to resources, services, information, and persons with influence everywhere in the world at levels unavailable to most of the earth's inhabitants. In spite of attempting to do otherwise, wherever the American Christian travels, he or she unintentionally represents an empire that is both loved and loathed around the world.

Citizenship and wealth were closely associated in the Roman Empire. While Paul does not appear to have been wealthy,[2] in contrast, American Christians are "rich Christians in an age of hunger."[3] While this wealth should, and often does, do tremendous good in the world, while wealth is an enormous resource for the work of the kingdom, it is also one of the most contradictory assets in the hands of the church.

Wealth provides such an envied position at the top of the pyramid, such power and status for those who possess it, that, according to Jesus, it is almost impossible for someone who has wealth to "enter the kingdom of God" (Matt 19:24). It is a miracle of God's redemptive power that makes freedom from wealth possible for the wealthy. The temptations for the wealthy are subtle and effective. Wealth makes Christians conservative, fearful, self-protective, and supportive of political policies that protect and reward the wealthy. At the same time, wealth enables the work of the kingdom to go forward.[4]

Like Paul, we American Christians have inherited and benefit from both the positive and negative resources of our respective empires. These blessings, which exist for the citizens, are available because of the ability of the empire to reward and punish, to make promises and threats, to win

---

2. Was Paul supported by wealthy patrons? There seems to be some evidence for this. It is clear that the generosity of wealthy Christians enabled Paul to live for extended periods of time without working. However, his insistence on self-support indicates he, unlike other itinerant teachers and philosophers, eschewed economic dependency on the wealthy and the restrictions and obligations inherent in the patron/client system. See Sampley, *Paul*, 124.

3. "By any objective criterion, the 5 percent of the world's people who live in the United States are an incredibly rich aristocracy living in the midst of impoverished masses" (Sider, *Rich Christians*, 27).

4. On the privilege and pitfalls of wealth in mission see Bonk's excellent book *Missions and Money* or my book *With Jesus in the World*.

friends and eliminate enemies. Many American Christians enjoying these blessings, in contrast to Paul, choose to remain ignorant about the nature of the empire of which we are citizens. We need to follow Paul's example and explore the empire of which we are part and the world that it shapes.

Explore Empire

We American Christians need to recognize that the apostolic mandate from Jesus for his followers gives us the opportunity and the responsibility to explore the features of the power and the glory of the American empire in the world. Like Saul, we are sent into the world with a vision that is no longer limited by our religious and national identity, or selective because of inherited bias, but rather a vision that is both realistic and hopeful. What we see around us in the world, however, is optional. Will we look the other way when we see the awful suffering, the lack of basic rights and living necessities, for so many in the world? Will we deliberately avoid eye contact with the inequalities and the injustice inherent in the free market, which rewards the privileged minority to which we belong?

We need to begin watching less news from sources that trumpet American superiority and begin listening to the brave prophetic voices of protest within and outside of America that question the self-congratulation of our political leaders. We must begin listening to the voices of the subjugated and shattered from everywhere in the world that contradict the rosy analysis of professional pundits and our own wishful thinking.

Let the American church explore the world at home and abroad in order to understand it. Rather than limit our travel to superficial and brief forays for vacation or short-term mission, we need to include travel in those parts of the world deemed unsafe and unfriendly for Americans. We American Christians can chose to travel like Jesus instructed his followers and as Paul demonstrated. We can choose to be hosted by local Christians and others, doing without professional paid staff of friendly people to serve our every need, anticipate our desires, and offer goods and services roughly equivalent to our privileged expectations. If we travel as Paul, we will discover the reality of the world beyond our perceptions shaped by personal bias, cultural pressure, or national interests.

In exploration, slow is good. Jesus and Paul probably never reached speeds beyond how fast they could run. The average speed of their travels was likely less than three miles per hour. Jesus and Paul walked, used donkeys, and sailed. This gave them time to relate to other travelers for days and weeks at a time, rather than just hours. They were reliant upon the generosity of others for their basic needs while traveling. They had time to listen to the hopes and the fears, not only of those on the same level as their own on the social pyramid, but of the people above and below them socially, especially of those below.

Just as Roman citizens traveled the Mediterranean and saw everywhere the demonstration of the validity of the pagan promises, so Americans traveling in the world today are often reinforced in their assumptions about the good of the American way of life that they enjoy. Paul spent enough time immersed in the pagan culture of the empire to recognize not only its strengths, but its dark sides, its broken promises, its overlooked human toll. We need to do the same. We need to spend time exploring the world among people who do not profit from giving us preferential treatment. But that is not enough.

Experiment with the Gospel

As Paul, we Western Christians have the opportunity to respond to the realities in the world of which we are aware by experimenting with the gospel in the global pagan empire. The easiest and least effective response by Christian explorers of pagan empires is to endorse and embrace the good and reject and condemn the evil in society. But this is a response that neither Jesus nor Paul demonstrated. Paul's experiments with the gospel in the empire was not driven by an agenda about the good and evil of the world, rather it began and ended with a complete and unwavering commitment to Jesus as the way, the truth, and the life for all people, pagan or Jew, male or female, slave or master. Commitment to the gospel of Jesus, rather than a reaction against the evils within pagan culture or an embracing of the good, set Paul's agenda.

Western Christians must always begin with commitment to Jesus and the good news of the kingdom when confronting either the dark or the dazzling sides of empire, for without a radical commitment to the gospel of Jesus, the proclamation tends to either become bombastic or domesticated, nasty or nice. Both are inauthentic representations of the gospel. Commitment to Jesus and the good news of the kingdom allows for creativity and experimentation. Experimentation involves the possibility and freedom of making mistakes.

This is the challenge of the present and the future. Whereas globalization is an extension of paganism, repackaged for the entire world, Christianity must be a clear alternative that connects to the lives, the hopes, the dreams, and the disappointments of the contemporary pagans who live in this global pagan empire. What is needed to be authentic representatives of the kingdom is a combination of living free of the pagan promises that shape America and the world and connecting the promises of the kingdom with those same pagan promises. This contradictory connecting makes effective representation of the gospel a risky and misunderstood venture. It necessitates constant adaptation and creativity. This is what caused Paul such massive and unrelenting controversy within the Jerusalem church, such animosity from the Jewish community, such reaction from and appeal to pagans.

The Voyage toward the Kingdom

Saul's encounter with Jesus affected his status. Like Jesus, Paul voluntarily abandoned his position of privilege and the power and the glory that accompanied it. His rights as citizen of Rome, his education, his natural abilities, his status in the Jewish community, all of these Paul considered "as rubbish" (Phil 3:8). Paul revealed Jesus' power and glory through his own weakness and shame rather than through his achievements and status. It is this voluntary identification with the weak and the shamed of the empire that made Paul like Jesus in the world. He revealed the astonishing nature of the good news from the position of Jesus. A final look at the diagram depicting the potential for Christians in globalization might be helpful.

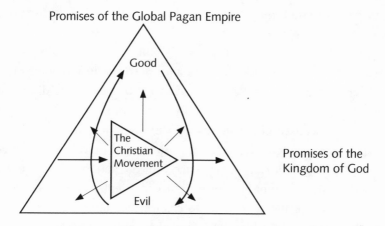

FIGURE 8.1. The Church as Movement of the Kingdom in the Global Pagan Empire

The social location of Jesus and of Paul was that of the early Christian movement as it swept through the empire, attracting adherents, gathering force, and challenging the status quo. This is the social location of almost every church in the world that is experiencing explosive growth today. It is the location that is forced on the church in nations with a hostile majority religion or ideology. This can also be the location of choice by Christians in the West, on both local and global levels.

The orientation toward the kingdom that shapes the authentic community of Jesus is impossible at the very top of the pyramid. There is simply no room for the alternative orientation toward the kingdom to fit unless it is aligned with the shape of the empire. The closer to the top the church is, the less of an alternative it can be. Conformity to the characteristics of the elite is inevitable if the church is the elite of the world. Power conforms and absolute power conforms absolutely.

Like Paul, we Christians are individually and collectively called to take on the form of servant and become obedient to the point of risking death on the cross, institutionally and personally, socially and physically, if we are to be authentic representatives of Jesus and the kingdom in the world. The exploration of the empire and the experimentation with the gospel within it must be from the lower social positions if we Christians are to discover the reality of the world we inhabit, and the occasions for connecting the good news of the gospel to the cultural patterns of good and evil.

As Paul demonstrates, just as it is not authentically Christian to seek or accept the position of power, status, and control at the top of the pyramid of empire, it is also not authentically Christian to seek to dismantle the pyramids of the empire directly. The power of the gospel to change the world is exercised in the alternative movement toward the promises and life of the kingdom. The alternative shape and movement, oriented towards the kingdom, runs interference with the patterns of society for the good of all whether or not this influence is accepted or appreciated.

The power of the good news to change individuals and society is made visible in the kingdom movement through the participants' good works that glorify God (Matt 5:14–16). The reality of the promises, the credibility, the attraction, the relevance, the immediacy of the good news of the kingdom, is to be made visible through the church. Just as invisible light is refracted in visible colors of all kinds, so the Christian movement, oriented toward the kingdom, is in the position to refract the light of Jesus, making it visible and distinct within the darkness of the glittering promises of the pagan global empire in every community and city in which it exists.

We Western Christians can view ourselves as participants in a growing movement toward the kingdom that at once crosses both the local and global patterns of good and evil. Our congregations should reflect this self-understanding. Institutional structure and programs should be for the purpose of creating and sustaining the momentum and for equipping the participants for representing the good news of the gospel in the world in ways that liberate and change individuals as well as human systems of good and evil. Paul's instructions to the congregations established through his efforts indicate that creating and sustaining the momentum of the movement are the only reasons for organization.

This understanding of organization should be normative, not only for every congregation, but for all organizations of which the congregation is part—regional, national, and international. As in the early Christian movement, these associations of congregations should have the features of a network, connected perhaps by traditions, creeds, and confessions, but more importantly, by vision and direction. These associations should be formed for relational, practical, and apostolic reasons in order to make the promises of the kingdom visible, credible, attractive, and effective in the world. Expanding and sustaining the growing Christian movement of the kingdom in the world is the agenda. Institutional power, status, and stability are not.

As Paul demonstrates and explains, status in this movement exists at the congregational and network level, but it is earned not by being above others, but by being ahead of others, demonstrating the life, teaching, and way of Jesus in the world in unusually clear and consistent ways. Status is earned through one's long-term commitment to the gospel of Jesus, and consistency in Jesus' way in every area of life. This kind of status is unrelated to ethnicity, gender, wealth, education, or other restrictors or enhancers of social status in the culture. Proximity to Jesus and the ability to represent the good news of the kingdom to others is the primary standard of status in the movement toward the kingdom.

Paul's example defines leaders as those who exercise authority in the movement, not by being credentialed or holding a powerful office within the organization, but by being recognized and affirmed by those in the movement as representing Jesus in their lives. Homelessness, suffering, sacrifice, shame, and voluntary poverty for the sake of the gospel are leadership credentials within the movement according to Paul, as is boldness, and demonstrating the transforming power of God in ones' life (Phil 3:10). Proximity to Jesus, the demonstration of his life, the embodiment of the good news of the gospel, are all bases of authority and status for leaders of the Christian movement in all areas, from congregational to global.

Like Paul's journeys, the Christian movement in the global pagan empire across both cultural patterns and time is sustained through the organization and exercise of human and spiritual resources for the journey. The integration and preparation for full participation of volunteers in the movement, both for those who join and those who are born to parents within the movement, is an ongoing enterprise. Not everyone in the kingdom movement has the gift of an apostle, but all participate in and contribute to the apostolic mandate of the movement by using the gifts that they have been given. The educating and equipping task within the movement is critical. Like Paul, the proven leaders of the movement have the responsibility to invite younger and inexperienced participants to accompany them, especially in the apostolic tasks of exploration and experimentation, task for which younger people are especially gifted. The calling of younger leaders is continuous. The call within the kingdom movement is not a call to "go" primarily, but a call to "come with," a call to accompany the leaders, as Timothy did with Paul.

Formal education, including university, seminary, and other graduate studies, needs to be designed to sustain, motivate, and expand the movement rather than to build and maintain institutions. Education is especially important in America, where academic resources are readily available and where education at all levels serves American global interests. Christian education can be a major contributor to the kingdom movement, sharing the leadership of the movement as scholars seek to understand the world and appropriate the good news of the kingdom in every area of the world.

The Christian movement, like Paul's life, is meant to be blessed and to bless all people through the abundant life of Jesus. The abundant life, which includes enduring shame, misunderstanding, ridicule, and hardships as well as freedom, joy, love, peace, and contentment in life, is the attractive distinction between the movement and the global empire in which it journeys. The life of the living Lord of all gives abundant life in the present and life forever in the future. The pagan promises of a life of abundance, enjoyment, and self-gratification are tired and empty in comparison.

Like Paul, we need to have the vision of the globalization of the good news of kingdom of God, the demonstration and proclamation of the power and the glory of the crucified, risen Lord in the world of fabulous wealth and grinding poverty, of SUVs and HIV, of wars and peace talks, of democracy and demagogy. Like Paul we need to regain an awareness and appreciation for the resilient church in the East and the dynamic church of the Southern Hemisphere, for "Christianity is flourishing wonderfully among the poor and persecuted while it atrophies among the rich and secure."[5]

5. Jenkins, *Christendom*, 220. This important book gives a thorough historical overview, statistics, ecclesiological descriptions, and predictions of the growth and development trends of the global church.

We American Christians are divided. The good and evil categories of culture have become the categories of the church. The contradictory agendas of conservatives and liberals have divided congregations into warring camps, American Christians from each other, and American Christians from Christians of other nations. Instead of being "obedient unto death," the church in the America has become, at least in some ways, disobedient unto spiritual death, a squabbling, irrelevant, and crumbling pyramid of past glory.

Paul's concern for unity across ethnic, social, and theological divisions is where we must begin if we are to recover the dynamics of the Christian movement. If Jesus was capable of dismantling the dividing wall between pagan and Jew in Ephesus, is not the power of Jesus adequate to dismantle the wall that divides Democrats from Republicans, liberals from conservatives, blacks from whites, and rich from poor? Power and positions must be subjected to the message of the gospel and the presence of the spirit of discernment among us.

A return to radical allegiance to Jesus, while crucifying the agendas, statuses, and prejudices that fragment the Christian movement into tiny clusters of allies fighting others in the church, is essential for beginning the recovery of the potential of the Christian movement. Paul is adamant about this to those who joined the movement. It is not that all congregations need to be unified to all other congregations; it is enough that each congregation be the staging grounds of a journey that begins with uniting for travel toward the kingdom. As internally diverse congregations begin anew the journey toward the kingdom they will be brought together with other congregations in the Christian movement. The tension will be creative.

The Voyage

The God of Scriptures is the God who calls his people forward toward the promise, toward life. The great travel document of Scripture depicting the successes and failures of those on the journey of faith through the empires of the world includes summaries of incredible sweeping clarity. Especially poignant is the faith chapter of Hebrews 11. "All these [biblical heroes of faith] died in faith without having received the promises, but from a distance they saw and greeted them. They confessed that they were strangers and foreigners on the earth. . . . If they had been thinking of the land they had left behind, they would have had opportunity to return. But as it is, they desire a better country, that is, a heavenly one. Therefore God is not ashamed to be called their God; for he has prepared a city for them" (vv. 13–16).

Without a doubt, Abraham and Sarah, Moses, and Paul had feelings of trepidation as they set out. Whenever people leave the familiar for the unknown, whether traveling by camel, on foot, on ships, or on airplanes, insecurity and anxiety build. Our feelings are the same as the biblical heroes of faith, for only the technology of the empires has changed through time. The biblical history of great pagan empires begins in Genesis and ends in Revelation. The American empire is located somewhere among the world empires of the past and future. We, like the biblical people of faith have two possibilities. We can either be loyal citizens and supporters of empires like Assyria, Persia, Egypt, Babylon, Rome, or America, or loyal citizens of, and pilgrims and strangers in the direction of the kingdom of God.

The Bible is a travelogue that informs and guides the journey of all people since Abraham who respond to God's call toward the promise of life. It is a book by and for travelers in pagan empires toward God's empire. It is for all of us on the same journey of faith, which makes God's love through Jesus known to the world, all the time, everywhere. It describes the road through the powerful and glorious empires, through history, toward the promise of the kingdom of God. The travelers of the biblical story traveled through powerful pagan empires, past the monuments that demonstrated the kingdom, the power, and the glory of the Pharaohs and Caesars. These participants on the journey toward the promise made the promises of God and the coming kingdom real, attractive, believable, and concrete.

How does an institution become a movement again? How does the church recover the momentum partially lost in the West since Constantine? How do the followers of Jesus actually follow on a journey toward the promise of life, abundant and eternal, toward the promise of the kingdom? The example of Paul in Acts and his instruction to the early Christian movement give us additional relevant guidance for the journey.

Traveling through the globalized empire of the future will be equivalent to traveling through the Roman Empire on the Mediterranean. The Mediterranean, the unstable, volatile, liquid world of ideas, promises, and images, exhibited power and glory that tantalized the have-nots and rewarded the haves. Like Paul, we American participants in the Christian movement must learn to be at home on this sea, to navigate safely through its winds, waves, islands, and coastlines of treacherous magnificence. We need to utilize its potential and recognize the limitations, flaws, and death in the American dominated, cyber-Mediterranean center of the pagan global empire in which we live.

Paul, drawing from his experience sailing the Mediterranean, writes to the Christians living in the great seaport city of Ephesus that they should not be as "children, tossed to and fro and blown about by every wind" (Eph 4:14). The culture of the empire resembled the sea at its center; the culture of the global empire today also resembles the sea. But like Paul, we must utilize the sea rather than avoid it. We must weigh the anchor and set sail with Paul to the ends of the empire that now includes the ends of the earth.

9

Navigating Globalization

Navigating

NEAR THE SHORES AND around the rocky islands of the Mediterranean, especially in the Aegean, countless ancient cargo ships are submerged. The wood of the hulls, of course, has mostly vanished and what remains for underwater archeologists or treasure hunters to discover are amphorae, special pottery jars designed to fit into the curved holds of a small cargo ships. If sealed, these amphorae still sometimes contain traces of olive oil, wine, and other products traded in the Mediterranean. Analysis of the contents of these amphorae and the clay from which they are made allows archeologists to trace the locations of the amphorae's origins and thus plot the trade patterns of the Mediterranean in specific eras. From the evidence it is clear that sea trade in the first century was a flourishing, lucrative—and hazardous—undertaking.

It was not that ancient seafarers were poor navigators. On the contrary, they were extraordinarily skillful, for they needed to navigate the hazards of voyaging along treacherous coastlines, jutting islands, and dangerous rocks submerged just beneath the surface of the water. And they needed to do this without navigational aids on shore and technology on the ship. It was the captain's experience and navigational wisdom learned from others' experiences that lowered the risk of shipwreck. Most of the time these first-century mariners were successful, but under certain conditions, such as storms that drove them into unfamiliar waters at night, their navigational skills alone would sometimes not suffice and the ship with its crew and cargo would be lost.

I remember the first time we sailed in the Mediterranean under those very shipwrecking conditions. We had made a long passage from Italy to Kalamata, on the southern tip of Greece, then on south to Kithira Island, where we had planned to rest and recover after several days and nights of continuous sailing. But as we arrived in Kithira we heard a rumor from other sailors that a major storm was moving in from the west. By the next morning the wind had picked up in the rather unprotected town harbor, creating enough surge inside to put all of the boats tied along the municipal wharf in danger of being damaged. Reluctantly but hurriedly we decided to leave immediately and head east toward the island of Milos, some eighty-two miles distant and the closest island with a safe harbor. This meant, we knew, arriving just ahead of the storm in the middle of the night in Milos.

By about 1:00 a.m., with the strong winds on the stern, we saw the first lighthouse on a smaller island opposite of the large, protected harbor of Milos. In the blackness of that stormy night, we began to navigate into the Milos harbor in search of an anchorage and protection. At 2:00 a.m. we were inside the harbor, slowly creeping towards a place to anchor. Getting our orientation from several navigational lights on shore, a good chart, a simple GPS unit, and a depth finder, we were able to find a perfect spot to anchor in complete darkness in that unfamiliar harbor.

Our relief and celebration that night was not because we were better navigators than those first-century captains who ran aground under similar circumstances. Rather, our success was due to the help from the onshore navigational aids and our modern instruments and charts aboard, just enough for us to safely find our way in the dark into a place we had never been before.

Navigational Tips from Paul

So it was for the churches in the seaports of the empire. Paul, the apostle who took the gospel from land to sea, the man of empire and kingdom, of Jew and Greek, learned how to navigate toward the kingdom through cultural and religious hazards of the empire. He then shared the wisdom he had collected through observation and experience with those who joined the movement of the kingdom. Like navigational aids ashore and charts aboard, the letters of Paul to the seaport churches lowered their risk of grounding, capsizing, or sinking while voyaging in the hazards of the Mediterranean culture.

Gleaned from Paul's example recorded in Acts and themes from his writings to the churches around the Mediterranean, the following are some navigational tips for pilgrims and strangers, explorers and experimenters in the movement toward the kingdom through global empire. This navigational wisdom applies to voyaging by faith toward the kingdom in the twenty-first century. These are principles that we continue to practice on our voyages on *SailingActs* in the Mediterranean.

1: Leave Jerusalem

When making a passage across open and unknown seas for a distant, unfamiliar port, the most difficult moment emotionally is when you untie the dock lines. The harbor has been so safe and secure, so close to help, so satisfying, that the prospect of facing certain but unknown challenges alone, of being uncomfortable and at times afraid, makes the simple task of untying the ropes an exercise in anxious resolve. We have been through this now a number of times but the feelings are always the same. In our heads we know that the boat is our home whether at sea or land, but our hearts get quickly and firmly tied to the security of harbors.

American Christians, living in the "ends of the earth," have, with the impressive permanence of our institutions, our cultural success, our predictability, and control, rebuilt Jerusalem in America. Jerusalem feels like home. But as Jesus made clear to his followers, Jerusalem is not home; Jerusalem is the place to start from. Our goal is not to return to the past. It is not to find a secure place in the present. Home is not a place at all. Home is the kingdom, already present but with future completion. Like Paul, we can be at home in the empire as pilgrims traveling toward the kingdom.

The orientation toward the present and future kingdom of God however, does not imply abandonment of those who deliberately choose to stay behind in the past, in Jerusalem, or in the empire. Paul attempted to maintain connections and relationships with those who refused to be changed, who stayed physically, emotionally, ethnically, theologically, and traditionally in Jerusalem. These connections, however, did not prevent Paul from moving ahead toward the kingdom, toward the future, via Rome.

Leaving Jerusalem will change us. As Saul left Antioch and returned later as Paul, those who leave on the journey of exploration and experimentation toward the kingdom never return the same. When they do return to where they started from, it is to share with those at home the good news of the power and the glory of the kingdom in contrast to the power and the glory of the empire. The changed leaders and pioneers of the movement lead the followers and participants of the movement toward the kingdom. The return of the changed explorers and experimenters changes the rest of the church, and all who participate in the Christian movement. This, I believe, is descriptive of Paul and Barnabas, and the church in Antioch (Acts 13:1; 14:26).

2: Take the Necessities

While taking plenty of food and water for a passage offshore is essential for life while voyaging on a sailboat, we know that if we run low we can replenish these along the way. Additionally, there are other items we carry on *SailingActs* all of the time, without which we cannot begin to sail in the Mediterranean at all and that cannot be obtained easily en route. These include our passports, boat registration documents, proof of insurance, and generally a ship's log. What are the necessities of the Christian movement?

Kingdom identity and tradition. Paul never forgot his personal identity. His identity as "the least of the Apostles" (1 Cor 15:9) always included the recognition of who he was personally before and after his encounter with Jesus. Paul also took his Jewish identity on his travels. Although he became "all things to all people" he did so with a deep appreciation for his heritage and identity as a Jew. As mentioned earlier, Paul saw God, himself, and the world in light of the stories of creation, the exodus from Egypt, and the rise and fall of the Israelite kingdoms.

Christians also share those stories, as well as those of our own particular traditions, good and bad. Take them with you on the journey. They may feel heavy at times, but these memories are like a keel of a sailboat, giving stability and enabling progress to be made in the storms at sea.

National identity, passport. Paul likely had a little document called a *diptych*, which he seemed to have forgotten on several occasions. Or perhaps he just kept it hidden, for although his citizenship gave him great privileges, he did not advertise it. Why? He recognized clearly that Rome, even though it offered protection, a common language, relative ease of travel on a system of fine roads and shipping connections, and political stability, making the journey with the gospel through the empire possible, Rome was still not the kingdom of God.

Like Paul, American Christians should possess valid passports and be ambivalent about their privileged status. Perhaps we should only utilize the power of citizenship and our passports when it benefits others. Like Paul, we should keep our national identity tucked away out of sight, but make sure everyone is aware of our citizenship in the kingdom of God.

Like Paul, American Christians are citizens of arguably the most powerful global empire in history. Citizenship allows American Christians to travel throughout the global empire on their way to the kingdom. This is a privilege and a responsibility. The majority of the participants in the Christian movement globally are restricted by politics and poverty from extensive movement. All American Christians who can afford a passport should have one, for we are citizens of a privileged nation in a desperate world. An American passport is a potential resource to be used for good in the world. Perhaps every congregation in America could give a passport to every person it baptizes, along with instruction to go into the world in order to share the good news of the kingdom. These are essential travel documents for American and kingdom citizens.

Vision. Paul's journeys were always made with a kind of "memory of the future," the Damascus Road vision of the power and glory of the living Jesus and the implications this has for living in the present and for the future of the world. Without a vision of the reality of the living Jesus and the kingdom, our own journey will degenerate into surviving, a wilderness wandering, or an aimless search for hope, meaning, and identity that convinces no one, including our own children, of its ultimate validity.

3: Welcome Everyone

One of the pleasures of living on *SailingActs* in the Mediterranean is the opportunity this gives to invite others aboard. We have hosted religious Jews, secular atheists, Muslims, and Greek Orthodox Christians. While these guests generally only spend several hours aboard, the conversations almost always tend, sooner or later, to take a religious turn, with lively debate on just about anything related to truth, God, or the world. Invariably, we all learn something new.

More significant are the guests who chose to come along for a day or more. On a sailboat, with no chance of escape from personal conflict, seasickness, or fear in a night storm, people learn to know each other, to bond, to cooperate, to appreciate each other in new ways. In a fairly short time, on a sailboat there is a kind of unity in diversity that is seldom experienced on land.

Paul's experience as a passenger on the small cargo ships that plied the coastal waters of the Mediterranean, collecting all kinds of people with a common destination, gave him insight into the nature of the church as a new kind of voyaging community. Neither the passengers aboard the cargo ships nor those who had joined the Christian communities were united because they were similar, but rather because they were on the same journey toward a common destination.

The church in globalization needs to take the unprecedented opportunity to welcome the stranger aboard for the voyage toward the kingdom. But it is not the diversity that makes this so clearly a demonstration of the kingdom of God, but the unity in the diversity. Our congregations should always seek to bring rich and poor, black and white, male and female, educated and illiterate, conservative and liberal, Democrat and Republican, together in creative tension, to learn how to cooperate on the voyage toward the kingdom. *E pluribus unum* is a public display of the promise of the future kingdom now.

4: Tack When Necessary

Most of the time it seems the winds in the Mediterranean have the un-canny ability to blow in precisely the worst possible direction for making progress. This is of course not true; there are favorable winds, but only if another destination had been selected. It is very rare indeed to make a run in a straight line for your destination in the Mediterranean. It is often necessary to tack, slowly gaining ground without moving directly toward the desired destination.

The routes in biblical maps that indicate the journeys of faith in, out, and through empires by Abraham, Moses, Jesus, and Paul were never in straight lines. The itinerary seemed to change constantly for these travel-ers of faith, but never the final destination. Paul's sailing experience of "go-ing with the wind" but eventually arriving at the original destination may have affected his philosophy of travel in the empire toward the kingdom. Side trips, deviations, lengthy waits, seasons of recovery, imprisonment, weather, and even dreams—all affected Paul's itinerary, but seldom his destinations, and never his orientation in life toward the kingdom and home.

Travelers through the global empire in the Christian movement need to be flexible, to constantly adjust their heading in response to shifting storms, to take advantage of the winds and waves of culture, and to re-spond to the wind of spirit, which like the wind in the Mediterranean, blows where it chooses (John 3:8). The destination of the kingdom, how-ever, is never what is to be adjusted. The destination determines the over-all direction.

5: Do Not Always Heed Warnings

This is sensitive and problematic advice. It has to do with taking risks wisely, but taking them just the same.

Leading up to an offshore passage in the Mediterranean, our days are filled with preparation. Collecting as much weather information as possible is one of these activities. There are a number of problems with this. The forecasts often contradict each other, so we joke about looking at enough forecasts on the Internet until we find the one we want, and then plan our departure accordingly. In spite of the forecasts, we almost invariably discover on the voyage that the weather is either substantially better or much worse than any of them predicted. While we still pour over the forecasts before leaving, we have learned to rely more on the advice of experienced sailors and locals and our own experience, and then to plan for any weather contingency.

Another issue we face sailing on the eastern end of the Mediterranean is the warnings from the US State Department on travel in regions of unrest. Sadly, this is more or less a permanent condition in some parts of the world, and staying away because of a perceived risk would mean never visiting some places. So we go anyway, but carefully, finding ways to lower any unnecessary risk.

Didn't both Jesus and Paul travel to Jerusalem despite the warnings? Were their choices to do so a mistake? On the voyage to the kingdom we must learn to consider and at times ignore travel warnings from the officials; their fear is irrelevant and antithetical to the apostolic journey, for the earth belongs to the Lord. Go where pagan marketers fear to tread. Walk where the military will not go. Travel in those areas where civil war, chaos, and violence are the daily experience of life for all, including the Christians. Go to the parts of cities and the world where life is difficult and dangerous.

Paul not only went to Jerusalem, but he traveled to many other dangerous places as well, to Pisidian Antioch, Lystra, and Iconium after he had been beaten, stoned and evicted, and to Rome at least once, where he faced the real possibility, and eventually the reality, of death at the hands of the Roman authorities.

Jesus leads a movement that contradicts not only the patterns of society, but sometimes the warnings of the State Department as well. Do heed the travel warnings of Jesus and Paul, for they have made the journey before.

6: Respect and Distrust Empires

The international sailors we meet on the Mediterranean are uniquely non-nationalistic. Perhaps this is because of their experiences of entering and departing the ports of the many the different countries around the world and especially around the rim of the Mediterranean. The Mediterranean, surrounded by three continents containing an amazing diversity of ethnic groups, languages, religions, and cultures, makes voyaging in that sea both uniquely challenging and rewarding. Many of these countries have been at war in the past and the memories and tensions linger. The mistrust some of these nations have for each other is taken out, it seems, on the sailors passing from one country to another. These sailors learn the skills of international diplomacy, how to comply with arcane and opaque maritime rules, and how to recognize and avoid corrupt or cantankerous officials.

But, as Paul discovered, it is these same nations that provide protection that can be called on for a rescue if needed. Their coastguards eliminate the threat of piracy.

Boats sailing in national waters usually fly two flags—the "courtesy flag" of the host nation on the starboard main mast spreader, and lower, from the stern of the boat, the flag identifying the boat's national identity is flown. The voyage toward the kingdom requires respect for the host country with the changing "courtesy flag" of the nation in which the Christian movement is occurring, with the flag of identity of the kingdom of God clearly and permanently visible.

Paul seems to have a realistic perspective on the Roman Empire; it is capable of doing relative good, but never consistently. Paul seemed to appreciate and comply with the empire to the extent it allowed and facilitated his work of the kingdom. However one thing is certain. No matter how much good the empire enabled Paul to accomplish for the kingdom, he never confused the Roman Empire with the kingdom of God. Neither should American Christians.

7: Keep Moving

When sailing in the Mediterranean, unlike crossing oceans, sailors have the option of harboring at night in some quaint harbor of a Greek village, on a remote island in the Aegean, dropping anchor along the picturesque southern coast of Turkey, or perhaps even spending a few days in a marina with a swimming pool and restaurants. The temptation to linger just a few days longer instead of pressing on toward the final destination sometimes delays the voyage so long that the planned port is never reached.

Or if, when underway, the wind dies and forward motion drops, the boat begins imperceptibly to drift off course. No matter how much one spins the wheel, a boat that is not moving fast enough cannot be kept on course. Forward movement is necessary to steer.

Paul also knew, as any sailor knows, that any ship making progress is constantly unstable. For the church at sea, faithfulness is not measured by stability, direct itineraries, solid budgets, and predictable programs, but rather by its faithful and hazardous following of Jesus who is the way, the truth, and the life. As Jesus taught, and as Paul demonstrated, looking back on the stable and successful individuals and institutions one leaves behind is antithetical to the life of the kingdom.

8: Test the Winds

The capricious nature of the winds in the Mediterranean demands constant decision making. Should I reef the mainsail now, or later? Should I change sails, or wait awhile to see if the wind will pick up or slack off? Should I just give up and start the motor?

The churches that Paul left behind in places like Corinth struggled to balance their ship in the sweeping changes that occurred as women spoke, freedom dominated, and chaos reigned. This struggle for balance marks the voyage of the church today. The temptation by some of the ship's crew to cast caution to the wind and hoist all sails in order to make as much progress as possible, regardless of the dangers, is often countered by others who fear imminent capsize. Balance between ballast and sail is necessary for both progress toward the kingdom and safety at sea.

The Greek word *pneuma* can be translated either as "wind" or "spirit," connoting unseen power. This power, whether of the natural wind experienced on a voyage at sea or spiritual winds on the voyage of faith, can be either dangerous or beneficial.

Paul became an expert at judging the winds of the Mediterranean, advising the ship's leaders to stay in the port on Crete, for instance, which they did not, with disastrous results (Acts 27:9–12). He also became skilled in judging other winds as well, the winds of cultural change, headwinds of resistance from his detractors, and spiritual winds that threatened to blow the nascent church off course (Eph 4:14).

For the church in America today, it is not always easy to distinguish between the winds of popular cultural issues and the winds of the Spirit. Like on the voyage of Paul that shipwrecked, winds that seem favorable may eventually push the church into violent storms or the doldrums. We must test the wind—"test the spirits"—as we sail (1 John 4:1).

9: Take the Anchor

At the end of the voyage to Rome on *SailingActs* we visited St. Agnes Catacomb, in which early Christians had expressed their faith in the resurrection by carving Christian symbols on the walls of the tombs. One of these symbols, used extensively by Christians living in other port cities of the empire, was a ship's anchor, representing the cross. In this particular one, there is an alpha (A) on the left and an omega (Ω) on the right of the anchor-cross. Those early Christians seemed to recognize that the beginning and the end of the voyage of faith on the church-ship is possible because of the anchor, Jesus.

As Paul demonstrated in his actions, Jesus provides security in instability. Jesus the anchor is portable security, providing a home wherever the boat spends time, but allowing the ship to continue the voyage, never a captive of a particular place. Like the story of the storm on the Sea of Galilee, it is the presence of Jesus that outweighs the fear of storms.

Sailing Home

Human effort since the beginning of history has been to control the sea-like world outside of Eden, to seek stability by organizing and controlling life, to build empires that promise abundance in life, and threaten death in order to achieve these promises. But followers of Jesus are on the sea, at home there, living fully and confidently the life of abundance. But we are not yet home. While we experience and share the promises of the kingdom in empire, we are voyaging with joy toward the fulfillment of these promises, following Jesus, as Paul, to the ends of the earth, to the end of the journey.

We last hear about Paul in Rome, the mighty city he had dreamed of visiting for so many years. The story in Acts of the great apostle who took the gospel from land to sea, from Jerusalem to Rome, from Jew to Greek, from male to female, from master to slave, ends with Paul living in the heart of the most powerful empire the world had ever known. But Paul is neither dazzled nor intimidated, for he had met Jesus and caught a glimpse of the future triumph of the kingdom of God.

Now in Rome, at the end of a long journey that began when he met Jesus, he also met the most powerful human in the world, the man who through the knowledge of good and evil had achieved the ancient promise of becoming a god, the Caesar. Was Paul impressed? Did he lose confidence? Not at all! Paul was certain that the journey that began when he met Jesus would end when he met Jesus again.

We leave Paul there in Rome, an undefeated prisoner of empire and ambassador of the kingdom, welcoming all who came to see him. The final words about Paul in Acts are words of triumph, for Paul, the man of sea and land, empire and kingdom, is still "proclaiming the kingdom of God and teaching about the Lord Jesus Christ with all boldness and without hindrance" (Acts 28:31).

May we, like Paul, boldly and without hindrance, sail with confidence on the unstable sea and uncertain future toward life, toward the kingdom, toward home.

Bon voyage!

Bibliography

Allen, Roland. *Missionary Methods, St. Paul's or Ours?: A Study of the Church in the Four Provinces*. Grand Rapids: Eerdmans, 1962.

Arnold, Clinton E. *Powers of Darkness: Principalities & Powers in Paul's Letters*. Downers Grove, IL: InterVarsity, 1992.

Ballard, Robert D., and Lawrence E. Stager. "Iron Age Shipwrecks in Deep Water off Ashkelon, Israel." 2002. Online: http//web.mit.edu/deeparch/www/publications/papers/ BallardEtAl2002pdf.

Barber, Benjamin R. *Jihad vs. McWorld: Terrorism's Challenge to Democracy*. New York: Ballantine, 1995.

Batey, Richard A. *Jesus & the Forgotten City: New Light on Sepphoris and the Urban World of Jesus*. Grand Rapids: Baker, 1991.

Berkof, H. *Christ and the Powers*. Scottdale, PA: Herald, 1977.

Bonk, Jonathan. *Missions and Money: Affluence as a Missionary Problem—Revisited*. Maryknoll, NY: Obis, 2006.

Braudel, Fernand. *Memory and the Mediterranean*. Translated by Allan Lane. New York: Knopf, 2001.

Brueggemann, Walter. *The Bible Makes Sense*. Atlanta: John Knox, 1977.

Cahill, Thomas. *Sailing the Wine-Dark Sea: Why the Greeks Matter*. The Hinges of History 4. New York: Nan A. Talese/Doubleday, 2003.

Carter, Warren. *Matthew and Empire: Initial Explorations*. Harrisburg, PA: Trinity, 2001.

Casson, Lionel. *The Ancient Mariners: Seafarers and Sea Fighters of the Mediterranean in Ancient Times*. 2nd ed. Princeton, NJ: Princeton University Press, 1991.

———. *Travel in the Ancient World*. Baltimore: Johns Hopkins University Press, 1994.

Chomsky, Noam. *Hegemony or Survival: America's Quest for Global Dominance*. London: Penguin, 2004.

Clow, Kate. *St. Paul Trail*. Norwich, VT: Upcountry, 2001.

Crossan, John Dominic, and Jonathan L. Reed. *In Search of Paul: How Jesus's Apostle Opposed Rome's Empire with God's Kingdom*. San Francisco: HarperSanFrancisco, 2004.

Hohenfelder, Robert L. "Caesarea Maritima." *National Geographic* 171 (February 1987) 261–79.

Hutchison, William R. *Errand to the World: American Protestant Thought and Foreign Missions*. Chicago: University of Chicago Press, 1987.

Bibliography

Jeffers, James S. *The Greco-Roman World of the New Testament Era: Exploring the Background of Early Christianity.* Downers Grove, IL: InterVarsity, 1999.

Jenkins, Phillip. *The Next Christendom: The Coming of Global Christianity.* New York: Oxford University Press, 2002.

Joubert, Stephan J. "Reciprocity and the Poor among the First Followers of Jesus in Jerusalem." In *Life and Culture in the Ancient Near East,* edited by Richard E. Averbeck, Mark W. Chavalas, and David B. Weisberg, 371–88. Bethesda, MD: CDL Press, 2003.

Kraybill, Donald B. *The Upside-Down Kingdom.* Scottdale, PA: Herald, 1978

Malina, Bruce J. "Daily Life in the New Testament Period." In *Life and Culture in the Ancient Near East,* edited by Richard E. Averbeck, Mark W. Chavalas, and David B. Weisberg, 355–70. Bethesda, MD: CDL Press, 2003.

Perrottet, Tony. *Pagan Holiday: On the Trail of Ancient Tourists.* New York: Random House, 2003.

Price, S. R. F. "Rituals and Power." In *Paul and Empire: Religion and Power in Roman Imperial Society,* edited by Richard A. Horsley, 47–71. Harrisburg, PA: Trinity, 1997.

Ramsay, William M. *St. Paul, the Traveler and Roman Citizen.* Revised and updated by Mark Wilson. Grand Rapids: Kregel, 2001 [1925, 1895].

Sider, Ronald J. *Rich Christians in an Age of Hunger.* Dallas: Word, 1990.

Stark, Rodney. *Cities of God: The Real Story of How Christianity Became an Urban Movement and Conquered Rome.* San Francisco: HarperSanFrancisco, 2006.

Stutzman, Linford. "Antonio Gramsci's Theory of Cultural Hegemony Applied to Evangelical Missions in Albania." PhD diss, Catholic University of America, 1997.

———. *Sailing Acts: Following an Ancient Voyage.* Intercourse, PA: Good Books, 2006.

———. *With Jesus in the World: Mission in Modern, Affluent Societies.* Scottdale, PA: Herald, 1992.

Wallis, Jim. *The Call to Conversion: Why Faith Is Always Personal but Never Private.* Rev. ed. San Francisco: HarperSanFrancisco, 2005.

White, Jefferson. *Evidence & Paul's Journeys.* Hilliard, OH: Parsagard, 2001.

Wink, Walter. *Naming the Powers: The Language of Power in the New Testament.* Minneapolis: Fortress, 1984.

Yoder, John Howard. *The Politics of Jesus: Vicit Agnus Noster.* 2nd ed. Grand Rapids: Eerdmans, 1994 [1972].